Praise for *What If?* and Dr. Steve Robbins

"Dr. Steve Robbins will open your eyes to seeing things you may never have seen before, in a thought-provoking and creative way. His engaging, inspiring, and passionate energy will take you on a life-altering ride, from which you will walk away a more self-aware, accepting, and gracious individual."

> —Linda Esparza—Area Human Resources Manager, Parker Hannifin Corporation, Aerospace Group, Hydraulic Systems Division

"From the first time I heard Dr. Robbins, I knew I could listen and learn from him over and over and over! The content he provides, along with his style and delivery, are nothing short of, simply put, amazing! His knowledge of the human brain, human behavior, and how it all works together to create inclusion is not only informative, it's fun to learn! He has definitely changed mindsets all over my organization starting at the top with our senior level executives! Dr. Steve Robbins is a true ROCK STAR!"

> —LaTricia Hill-Chandler, CDE, Office of Global Culture, Diversity & Inclusion, Walmart Inc.

"Some people view life as a glass half-full. Some people view life as a glass half-empty. Dr. Steve Robbins will have you viewing the glass of life completely differently and from all angles by challenging you to think more lightly about yourself and more deeply about the world. His incredible sense of humor, exceptional storytelling, deep knowledge, and captivating personal story enable you to grow as a person, professional, and leader. He will compel you to rethink your view of the world. In the end, there is no choice but to become more enlightened by his teachings."

> —R. Matt Davis, President of Dow North America & Senior Vice President of Global Corporate Affairs

"Dr. Steve Robbins is an artful storyteller who blends a witty delivery with compelling content to drop serious knowledge about the neuroscience of unconscious bias and its effects in an insightful and memorable way. He's revolutionizing the way corporations approach inclusion and diversity programs by challenging us to rethink everything we thought we knew about this work—ultimately leading to a paradigm shift from compliance mandates to results-oriented transformational change. Through the power of curiosity, Dr. Robbins is helping us recognize and mitigate the negative effects of noise, outsiderness, and the social pain of exclusion by fostering a culture that is more empathetic and inclusive of all."

—Kevin J. Frazier, Senior Director, Global Culture, Diversity & Inclusion, Walmart Inc.

"Dr. Steve Robbins' powerful message and storytelling reminds us of the importance of an inclusive work environment. Backed by a deep knowledge of behavioral science, he encourages us to always be mindful of our employees' basic needs—to be part of a team and to be valued. Failing to establish an inclusive environment threatens our ability to be innovative. In a very complex healthcare environment, innovation is the only way we can differentiate ourselves from our competitors and retain and attract top talent."

—Karina Norr-McPhillips, MS, SPHR, SHRM-SCP, VP, Human Resources, Northwell Health

"Dr. Steve Robbins is an inspiring and passionate man who delivers his talks with high energy. Through a combination of science, humor, and wit, he captivated over 200 attendees at our Global Sales Meeting and was given a 5 out of 5 star review. He is able to connect incredible insight on human behavior to practical examples in the workplace and demonstrates how being open-minded is central to supporting and benefiting from the diversity in our organization."

—Kate McManus, VP Marketing, Delicato Family Vineyards

What If?

SHORT STORIES
TO SPARK INCLUSION &
DIVERSITY DIALOGUE

10th Anniversary Edition

Steve L. Robbins

nb

NICHOLAS BREALEY
PUBLISHING

BOSTON • LONDON

This edition first published in 2018 by Nicholas Brealey Publishing
An imprint of John Murray Press

A Hachette UK company

23   22   21   20   19   2   3   4   5   6   7   8   9   10

Author photograph on page 97 courtesy of Steve L. Robbins.

A CIP catalogue record for this title is available from the British Library.

Library of Congress Control Number: 2018908493

Paperback ISBN 978-1-4736-9054-7
US eBook ISBN 978-1-4736-9835-2
UK eBook ISBN 978-1-4736-9836-9

Printed and bound in the United States of America.

John Murray Press policy is to use papers that are natural, renewable, and recyclable products and made from wood grown in sustainable forests. The logging and manufacturing processes are expected to conform to the environmental regulations of the country of origin.

John Murray Press Ltd
Carmelite House
50 Victoria Embankment
London EC4Y 0DZ
Tel: 020 3122 6000

Nicholas Brealey Publishing
Hachette Book Group
53 State Street
Boston, MA 02109, USA
Tel: (617) 263 1834

www.nbuspublishing.com

Contents

CHANGING THE ORGANIZATION

Preface

Wow! It's been 10 years since the original edition of this book made it to print. My publisher tells me the book has done very well. Maybe that's why this second edition gets a chance at making an impact on readers' minds and hearts. Thank you to all who purchased the original and have supported me as I continue to do the work of inclusion and diversity. Right now, I bet some of you noticed I didn't write "diversity and inclusion." There's a significant reason for the switch. Some folks reading this will have a quick, involuntary negative reaction to the change. Many won't notice, and some won't care. There will be people who agree wholeheartedly with putting inclusion first and diversity second. Let me offer some of my reasoning for why inclusion should come before diversity.

A little background: Since the last edition, I have engaged with the work of inclusion and diversity through extensive study and exciting interactions with clients from all over the world. I have the benefit of coming at the work of inclusion and diversity from the perspective of a social scientist. Many of you know I am a big Michigan State University (Go Green!) supporter, having earned my master's and doctorate from its prestigious Department of Communication Science. Fundamentally, I was trained in the art and science of studying human behavior. If you know anything about the field of communication science, it's a relatively new field that grew out of two better-known fields, psychology and sociology. It may be easier to understand if I say that I am a social psychologist who looks at human communication. Moreover, over the last couple of decades, beginning shortly after graduating Michigan State, I took strong interest in the study of the brain and how it processes messages. The catalyst for my interest in the brain grew from trying to understand the factors that may have led my mom to take her own life in 1991. Fundamentally I was asking, "How did external and internal messages have such a negative and devastating impact on my mom? I have since accumulated a lot of knowledge in my brain about the human brain, and so I come at the study of human behavior (and inclusion and diversity) with the additional lens of a cognitive neuroscientist. The myriad perspectives that I bring to bear on inclusion and diversity have led me to believe that we put the proverbial cart before the horse. Inclusion necessarily comes before diversity.

Some people think of me as a "diversity expert." I'll be the first to admit I am not such. If I am an expert in anything, it's in human behavior, and I more consider myself a lifelong student of human behavior. In a sense, all of us are students of human behavior, as the human brain is constantly trying to make sense of the world it inhabits, a world with human beings interacting on a daily basis. I just happen to have formal training in it. I examine many aspects of human behavior. In the process I've learned many things. It just so happens that many of the things I've learned can be applied to an area some call "diversity and inclusion." One significant "aha" for me that I have come to firmly believe is that "diversity," which I define as when you have more than one person in the room, is nothing, even problematic, if there is no underlying foundation of "belonging" or "inclusion." Thus, I am an inclusion guy first. Do not interpret that statement to mean that I believe diversity is less important than inclusion. I highly value both inclusion and diversity. However, without an environment that breathes inclusion, we take the breath out of diversity. Put differently, inclusion unleashes the power of diversity. Exclusion is diversity's Kryptonite. Consider a relatively homogeneous group of people who don't get along. What do you think might happen if you inject "diversity" into that group? From an organization performance lens, what you have just done is introduce smart, talented, and skilled people with different experiences and perspectives into an environment that resists them and often blames them for disrupting the organizational order. Increasing "diversity" numbers might look good, but without a supportive inclusive foundation, the research suggests the "diverse" others you parachute in will suffer what researchers call "social pain."

Yes, current neuroscience research offers a clue as to why those who feel excluded often feel more tired, more anxious, and less productive. Being an outsider without a tribe that values you will light up pain circuitry in your brain. Ouch! Some well-meaning leaders (and "diversity" practitioners), unarmed with the current science that concludes that human beings are hardwired to belong, can actually do more harm when they attack issues of diversity without softening up the beachhead with inclusion. If an organization truly values diversity, it would cultivate a culture of inclusion so that the numbers don't turn people into superficial statistics. Doing inclusion right helps one to rightly do diversity.

Please read this new edition with the new lens of "Inclusion and Diversity." The 10 new stories come from that perspective. The original stories will also gain new interpretational life with a more updated, twenty-first-century lens. As with my keynotes and workshops, I've tried to keep the stories interesting with a sprinkle of science here, a pinch of emotion there and a good dose of humor throughout. You'll hear a little about my kids, who are no longer kids. As of this writing, my oldest (Nick—no longer Nicholas) graduated with a degree in actuary science but chose to follow his mission-oriented heart to teach math overseas. He has a master's in education from that other major university in Michigan. My second son (Zach—no longer Zachary) earned a full-ride scholarship to play golf at a NCAA Division I university and is enjoying his time as a student athlete. My third son (Jake—no longer Jacob) will be headed to the best university in the world, Michigan State, to pursue a career in science. If I have a favorite kid, it would be Jacob because of his choice of MSU. Just kidding! It's because he's 6'2" and can dunk a basketball. The youngest, my daughter (Natalie—still Natalie), now has her driver's license and finds ways to verbally and nonverbally remind me that I am now the shortest person in our family. I fire back by quoting a line by Mark Twain in response to tall people commenting at his short stature: "I feel like a dime among pennies." Hah! My beautiful wife continues to light up my heart and mind as my best friend as she teaches me how to be a better parent. It's a tough job for her but she's a trained educator! It's going to be a different world for us as pieces of our Robbins tribe are pushing forward to eventually form their own family tribes, but we look forward to spending more time traveling. On our bucket list is to be in attendance at all four of the majors in professional tennis. We've gone multiple times to the US Open in the great city of New York (actually Flushing Meadows). If anyone out there has connections to get us tickets to Wimbledon, the Australian Open, and the French Open, I'm right here!

So, thanks for all your support. I hope to see you during my travels and attempts to spread the message about inclusion AND diversity, but mostly about the power of caring for people, especially those you may not initially find to be much like you. If I happen to be a speaker at your organization or at an event that you also happen to be attending, please say hello. It's always good to have a tribe that cares about you. And especially a tribe that might have members who can get us into some major tennis tournaments!

Acknowledgments

Thanks to the many people I've encountered along this journey for your continued support and encouragement. I couldn't do this without all of you. There are many I have met along the way who have helped me to learn and build experiences that I can use to spread the message about the importance of belonging (inclusion) and of caring about others. I express my gratitude to you for your kindness and also for inviting me into your respective spheres to share my message. I'd like to name all of you, but I don't have the space to do so. And as I am now a bit older, I'm fearful that the neurons that once held all your names have either been purged or cannot be easily accessed without some trigger. If you do not see your name here, just know that I have heartfelt thanks to all of you who have invited me into your tribe, at least temporarily.

Thanks to...

My brothers from another mother, Tod, Mark, and Joe for being my tribe when I was temporarily in need of one. And, of course, thanks to

Sharon Wyn, that "other mother" for taking me in as a son when my mom passed.

My wonderful hardworking team at S2S Studios: Carese, Alyson, Sara Jo, and Mallory. They are aligned with my personal mission and put passion into the work of visual storytelling to make the world a better place.

All my Spartan homies in the Communication Department at Michigan State University, past and present. I could not be where I am today without the support of the people there, especially those who were my tribe that first semester when my mom passed. A specific shout-out goes to the late Dr. Chuck Atkin and the effervescent Dr. Bill Donohue. My mentors, even though they may not have known the impact they had on me.

My friends from my high school days who continue to support me even when contact is not regular, Dennis, Todd, and Craig.

The folks at Nicholas Brealey Publishing, especially to Alison and Michelle for putting up with my tardiness. I hope my stories make you laugh.

I must thank my family for putting up with a husband/father who was not always home like a "traditional" father. To my kids, I hope you will see past my faults and know that I continue to learn to be a good father. It's been difficult to know what to do in many situations since I did not have a father figure growing up. Well, I did, but he was not one I would want for any kid. Nicholas, Zachary, Jacob, and Natalie, please know that I love you and will always be there for you. To my wife, Donna, thank you for your patience, even-keeled demeanor, and enduring love. I know my travels make it feel like you are a single mom at times. I am looking forward to spending the rest of our lives together. Also, to my wife's mom (Connie) and family for being there and putting up with the little Vietnamese inner-city kid. Thanks to Rita especially for being the older sister I never had. And yes, I love you too, Mary, Ann, and Gary.

Thanks to you and your families for making family gatherings a reminder of why having a family is so important.

Finally, and mostly, thank you to my Lord and Savior Jesus Christ, who died on the cross for one such as me. It is by the power and grace of your unfailing love that I am still alive today. You stand for me, so there is none who can stand against me. Thanks for allowing me to be your servant, even with my many stumbles along the way.

My Story

As I continue to travel around the globe working with various organizations and businesses, I am often asked if I get tired of doing this work—of
this thing some have called "diversity and inclusion." My response is a
balanced one. "Yes and no," I say. The travel and being away from my
family are always difficult. And some of the people I encounter in my
travels just don't seem willing or able to embrace the idea that they actually live in a diverse world with diverse perspectives. They can't seem to
give up old twentieth-century patterns that don't work so well in the
twenty-first century. People like that can at times make the work
tiresome.

So, on the one hand, yes, I do get tired. On the other hand, I do not.
I am energized and sustained by the caring people I meet who support
me in this life calling that became clear to me in a crucible of cruelty. It
is from that crucible that I get my sustenance and passion for this work.
So let me tell you that story.

I immigrated to the United States in 1970. In the midst of

an escalating war in Vietnam, my mother married an American serviceman—not because she loved him, but so that she could bring me to the United States. Let me give you a little context for how difficult that decision was for my mom, for not only was she deciding to give her son a chance, but she was also simultaneously deciding to leave her family behind.

In Vietnamese culture, family is revered and valued. Family defines who you are, why you exist. Vietnamese people don't just say we value family. We actually do it! Family in Vietnam is not just Mom, Dad, and the kids the way we in the United States tend to think of it. The elderly aren't sent away. They are taken in. We don't get upset if a relative drops in unannounced. We break out the *pho* (beef noodle soup)! Family bonds are strong.

So when my mother chose to leave her family behind to ensure that her young son would have life, it was an excruciating decision for her. (Note that I did not say "have a life." The threat of death was an everyday reality.) She left her mother and father, her five brothers and sisters, and a bunch of aunts and uncles and cousins. She packed very little (because we had very little) and, with her five-year-old son in tow, traveled literally halfway around the globe to another world.

When we arrived in Los Angeles, I am sure my mom was thinking she had made a mistake.

When we got off the plane and walked into the airport, people were spitting on us. They were throwing things at us and yelling horrible words. I didn't understand English at the time, but even as a five-year-old, I could tell that the verbal bullets being fired at us came from a place of ignorant, misguided hate. What had we done besides accept America's offer of hope, freedom, and opportunity? If it seems unbelievable that some in this country would do such things to those only seeking refuge from death, consider the many tales from Vietnam veterans detailing their mistreatment upon returning to the country they had proudly and honorably served. If some could so mistreat their own heroes, imagine being Vietnamese during those years. I suppose the way my mother felt is much like how many immigrants feel today in a climate of protectionism, nationalism, and manufactured fear. Standing about 4'11" and speaking with a heavy accent, my mom was a convenient target for unwarranted discrimination, intentional exclusion, and painful ridicule. These injustices invaded her life with regularity, and there was little she could do about it.

The neighborhoods we lived in were not very nice to me, either. Many times I would come home covered in blood from fights. Some fights I started. Others I did not. Many occurred because I was the different kid with slanty eyes from the war. I was called "VC" (Vietcong), "Jap," "Chink," and worse. I was none of those. As the saying goes, "kids can be cruel."

Following these brawls I would find my way to our apartment, where my mom would pull me into her arms and hold me tight for minutes on end. She rarely said anything as she wiped the blood from me with a warm wet cloth. She didn't have to—the tears streaming down her face said it all. She was in much pain. I really didn't understand what my mom was going through on these occasions. I think I do now. With the privilege of raising four of my own children with my wife, I more deeply feel the grief she must have felt as she sent me to school in the morning, wondering how much blood would be on me when I returned from school in the afternoon. I cannot think of anything much worse than having to watch one's own kids suffer.

My mother thought she had brought us to a better place, and in many ways, she had. Undeniably, the United States was a much better place to be in than Vietnam at the time—but it wasn't the place she had been told about. It didn't live out the concept she held in her head. It didn't make a reality of "We hold these truths to be self-evident…that among those rights are life, liberty, and the pursuit of happiness."

Little by little, the injustices chipped life away from my mom. The man she married turned out to not be the coolest guy. He forced my mom, raised with Catholic influences, to have an abortion. I still remember the day we went to the hospital for the procedure. I didn't know what was happening; I just recall going to the hospital with my mom emotional and visibly distraught. When we left, she once again had tears running down her gentle face. When I later found out why we had gone to the hospital, I was filled with an unforgettable pain and anger.

For many reasons, I was never close to my stepfather, that uncool guy. It's difficult to become close to someone who beats you when you're one minute late for dinner, and then beats you again for not finishing the dinner you couldn't eat because you weren't hungry from the first beating. But he found a way to be close to my sister, Diane, his flesh-and-blood daughter. In 1984, he was convicted of sexually assaulting her. To this day, I still do not know when his awful offenses began; I just know they resulted in my sister's running away from home with a friend in the summer of 1985, when she was 13 years old. Later that summer, my mom received a phone call that would devastate her.

By that time, we had moved to Washington State in pursuit of jobs and to escape some of the hate we had endured. The man on the other end of the line, a King County sheriff's detective, delivered the horrible news that the girl my sister had run away with had been found murdered in the Seattle area. The detective said he believed that this girl's death was linked to a string of unexplained deaths of young women in that area, known as the Green River killings. When my mom asked about my sister, the detective could offer only a glimmer of hope: "We have been unable to locate your daughter, Mrs. Robbins." I remember my mom falling to her knees, sobbing so hard that her body shook violently. Though there was a chance my sister was still alive, most likely in grave condition, I think my mom knew her family was now short one life. I knew it, too.

That fall I headed back to college in Michigan with a heavy heart, weighed down by the knowledge that I likely would never see my sister again and the pain of knowing that my mom was suffering so greatly. Within my mother's small frame was the strongest woman I had ever known, will ever know. But no amount of strength could lift the enormity of the hurt that crushed her spirit every hour of every day. She did her best to mask that pain when we talked on the phone, but sometimes there was no hiding it. No one knew it at the time, but in the solitude of my dorm room that year heavy tears often flowed from my eyes. There were many late nights in which I sat alone in the dark, rocking back and forth, not knowing what to do for my mom, what to do for myself. At times, I didn't know if I could make it one more day. It is by the grace of God that I continue to see sunrises.

My mom tried to take her own life in 1989. I had no knowledge of this until recently when a friend from Washington showed me a videotape of my mom on a Seattle-area television program. It was a program about parents who had lost a child. On the videotape was a dispirited woman visibly distressed by the cumulative events of her life. The woman on the screen was my mom—but she was not. Asked about how she coped day to day, she told the program host that she continued the struggle for one reason only—her son.

The next two years were difficult for my mom, I'm sure, but she never let on, always protecting me from the pain that wreaked havoc on her emotional, spiritual, and physical being.

June 1991 was a wonderful, happy time etched into my life and, I suspect, into my mom's life, too. That's when I married my wife, Donna, a stunningly beautiful woman inside and out who filled gaps in my life, many unknown by me at the time.

My mom and Donna hit it off right away, though from casual observation they looked to be very different. A mental picture of their first meeting sticks with me. My mom is embracing my future wife with the kind of hug often reserved for long-standing family members and friends. It's kind of an odd scene, this tiny dark-haired Vietnamese woman locked together with a six-foot blonde who would one day be her daughter. It would take nearly 15 years before I recognized how that meeting would come to symbolize the work that I do.

Five months after my wedding, I was thick into my graduate studies at Michigan State University when I received a phone call from my mom back home in Washington State. We shared the events of our lives that past week. I don't recall the specifics. Before ending our conversation and hanging up, my mom softly said, "Long, you have Donna to take care of you now. I love you very much." I told my mom I loved her, too, and looked forward to our next phone call. But the next phone call from Washington State was not from my mom.

A little more than a week later, the phone rang. Donna answered and, following a brief conversation, handed the phone to me. I could tell something was terribly wrong. Sitting on the bed in our room, I found myself speaking with an officer from the Benton County Sheriff's Department. He asked if I was Steve Robbins and if I knew a woman named Nancy Robbins. "Yes," I said, "that's my mother." Thoughts, many unsettling, were running through my head at that moment as a brief silence fell.

"Mr. Robbins, I am sorry to have to tell you, but we just found your mother."

"Is she okay?" I asked.

"I'm sorry, sir, but your mother was found in her bathroom and she was not alive." Shaking, I asked what happened. "Apparently your mother took her own life. She had hanged herself from the showerhead."

I could not say anything as the weight of the pain crushed my vocal cords and my spirit. I shook as the tears drowned my eyes and a lifetime of events, good and bad, raced through my mind. I really don't recall much after that. I do remember the waves of pain that rocked my body.

A few days later I was in my mother's apartment sifting through her belongings, trying to comprehend what had happened, what was happening. Many questions drummed through my head. Why did my mom choose this path? Why didn't I see the signs? Why wasn't I there for her? The answers were nowhere to be found. The questions only ignited more questions, and my quest to answer them tormented my sleepless nights.

The more I thought about what my life would be like without my mom, the more I began to reflect on what my life had been like. Many experiences long silent in the deepest depths of my mind surfaced. Not all were pretty. I came face to face with the reality that I did not like myself much. More specifically, I did not like being Asian, being Vietnamese, being me.

More questions busied my thoughts. How does someone who looks like me get the name *Steve Robbins*? Why do I have a perm? Why have I had a perm since junior high? How come I can find Asian women attractive but have never been inclined to date one? In a different context, these questions might have been a bit funny. In this particular context, they burdened my soul. Recognizing that you've spent a lifetime suppressing large parts of your true self is powerfully painful.

After my mom's burial, I returned to Michigan with more questions than answers. A chapter in my life had been closed, and new ones were about to begin. At the time I did not know what would be written on those future pages. I just knew I had to press on.

As I look back today, I see how the painful experience of my mom's death shaped who I am and what I do now. It was her death that led me to become more interested in and sensitive to issues of inclusion and diversity. Her suicide directly influenced me to study how we talk to ourselves, our internal talk (intrapersonal communication), and ultimately led me to study the human brain. It also led me to a deeper self-examination—one that would tear scabs off old wounds but would also lead me to the core of who I am, of who my mom taught me to be. I would come to understand and put a label on the hate I had for myself. In the world of race studies, it is called "internalized racism." I hated myself because the messages I encountered in the world taught me to hate myself. Those messages created a negative mental model of people like myself. I had internalized the many negative messages about Asians, and specifically about Vietnamese people.

The many people who discriminated against my mom and me I remembered to be white. That did not teach me to hate white people. Far from it, it taught me to want to be white because white people were not being discriminated against. As I came to more fully understand what was happening, I also came to appreciate who I really was (and am) and what my mom had been trying to teach me all along about my heritage and history.

To be honest, I am still dealing with internalized racism today. I suspect I will be dealing with it for the rest of my life. But that's okay. I better understand the "dis-ease" within me now and how it plays out in society. I also understand what I've been called to do. All my past experiences, good and bad, beautiful and ugly, have equipped me to do the work I do around inclusion and diversity.

My mom sacrificed 26 years of her life to make sure that I could have life. She faced cruelty many times, too many times, during her short 47 years on this planet. I am certain she was not the only one. Many others face similar pain today. The reality of people needlessly suffering fuels the work I do.

When I go out to speak and to work with organizations, my motivation is a bit selfish. You see, I want people to understand that the work around inclusion, diversity, and cultural competency is not about political correctness or a better bottom line. Neither is it about compliance or protecting against a lawsuit. It's not even about changing demographics. No, at its core this work is about caring about other people, treating them with dignity and respect because they are human beings who deserve such. It's about standing up for justice in the face of injustice. It's about standing up for those who have been told to stand down.

I believe the negative baggage around "inclusion and diversity" was created and is carried forth by people who are blind, at least partially, to the myriad realities of our world, and who have not fully realized that doing the work of inclusion and diversity is truly about being a nice, caring, and compassionate citizen. It's about creating a sense of belonging for those who yearn for belonging. It's my guess that the vast majority of people would like to be called nice, caring, and compassionate. A large part of my work is to urge, encourage, and teach others to walk the talk of being nice, caring, and compassionate. If more of us would sincerely and genuinely do that, our world would be a much better place—a world where fairness and justice would rule, a place in which we cared for our neighbor even when our neighbor doesn't look like us, a neighbor from a half a world away.

I do this work to honor my mom and little sister, and to do my part in making sure that fewer people face what my mom faced. Why? Because I imagine that if, while my mom was alive, more people had stood up for justice, as a shield between her and injustice; if more people had protected her from the cruelty of ignorant and unmindful people; if more people had said, "You can't do that to her because she is a human being who has been given unalienable rights that supersede politics"; if more people had done those things in the midst of my mom's tears and my sister's suffering, I know that my four children would have a grandmother and an aunt to play with today. No, this work is not about numbers and statistics; this work is about real lives that suffer every day from the social pain of exclusion.

So, I do this work because I know firsthand the mountaintops and valleys of our world, and I want more people to experience the mountaintops. I can't and don't want to do this work alone, so I go out to touch people so that we can work side by side to make this a better place, especially for the generations to come.

Yes, I know this all sounds very idealistic and pie-in-the-sky, but as Dr. Martin Luther King Jr. so eloquently said, "I've seen the mountaintop," and it's a wonderful place. Let's all work together to be path makers, creating many paths to the mountaintop. It will be hard, painful work, an uphill battle littered with unbearable mind-sets and seemingly insurmountable circumstances. Yes, it will be that and likely more. There will be times when you will want to give up. I have experienced those times on many occasions. In those times, do what I do: I imagine my mom sitting on the floor telling my four kids the wisdom-filled stories she told me as a kid, and as she finishes she gives them all a great big hug. Before they all get up to leave, my mom tells my children to love and take care of each other, and to be path makers, not path blockers.

There is a Chinese proverb that says, "Tall trees face strong winds." I invite you to be a tall tree with me. Read the stories in this book within the context I have given you. Share them with others to spark inclusion and diversity dialogue. Practice curious and crucial conversations. Take advantage of teachable moments. Do all this and more to become a "tall tree," and when the strong winds hit, know that there are other tall trees in your presence. You may not see them, but they are there working around you, with you, and for you. And I am one of them. You are never alone in doing this good work. Good work is never done alone.

Ready?

Introduction

The stories in this book are meant to inspire you to see your world a little—or even a *lot*—differently. To get the most out of them, read them with an open mind and a willingness to entertain new perspectives. If there are times when you want to say, "No, it's not that way," pause and consider the book's title: *What If?* Ask yourself what if it *could be* that way? Temporarily suspend your current reality and imagine a different one, perhaps one even more different from what I have suggested.

After you have spent some time reading the stories, think about how the concepts apply to your daily life—at home, at work, and with your family and friends. Talk with others about how the stories can be used to create an environment of continuous learning. You will find that the stories present concepts beyond those of inclusion and diversity. They touch on many aspects of fundamental human behavior. Organizationally, they can provide many insights into the building blocks of a productive workplace, including leadership and mentoring, creativity and innovation, and organizational culture and engagement. And they explore how to effectively engage a global world increasingly defined by encounters with new people, new ideas, and new things.

This book will help you to be more cognitively flexible and behaviorally adaptable. If this sounds inviting to you and your organization, here are a few general suggestions to get you going. (In addition, there are specific questions, activities, and assignments at the end of each chapter.)

- Hold a series of brown-bag lunches to discuss the stories. Schedule the series strategically, ideally following a diversity-related organizational event so that you can continue the momentum.
- Emphasize continuous learning in your work team by using the book as common reading for each member of the team. In your regularly scheduled team meetings, spend 15 to 20 minutes discussing one of the stories. You will likely find that the stories spark other conversations beyond inclusion and diversity.
- Use the stories in your organizational newsletter. If you have a newsletter specifically devoted to inclusion and diversity, that's even better—definitely incorporate a story. (Remember to get permission from the publisher, Nicholas Brealey Publishing.)
- Use the book as common reading within your inclusion and diversity council and affinity groups. This can help stimulate discussion of various issues and opportunities.
- Get the organization's leaders to read the book or, at a minimum, to read selected stories from the book. The stories will give them different lenses through which to see inclusion and diversity, whether or not they currently "get it." The goal here is to reframe inclusion and diversity as a twenty-first-century issue that needs to be kept alive in their leadership meetings.

- Use the book as a catalyst for practicing storytelling and "story listening." It's interesting how much we can learn about our world and ourselves when we are asked to tell our stories and listen to the stories of others. Stories create context for others to understand us and for us to understand others and, maybe more importantly, ourselves.

- Use these stories as part of a mentoring relationship to spark dialogue and share experiences both inside and outside your organization. You will find that we are all on a journey of learning, and we are all at different places along the path. Everyone has something to share, a perspective worth hearing.

- You may find that you want to journal your thoughts as you read each story. It can be very rewarding to look back and see how your thoughts have progressed, your lenses have broadened, and your awareness has heightened. Use the stories to help you recognize and eliminate subtle (and not so subtle) slights that serve to devalue, exclude, and invalidate the stories of other people.

- Write your own stories!

REFRAMING
THE
WORLD

"Be less certain. Be more curious."
—**Steve L. Robbins**

| 1 |

The Right Environment

There is a small pond on our property that provides my family with all sorts of fun. In the winter, it's a makeshift skating rink that allows me to prove—over and over again—that humans were not designed to maneuver on ice, nor should two sharp blades be attached to shoes and used as a mode of travel. Come summer, after the bruises have faded from my rear, the pond transforms into a delightful fishing hole.

When the pond was created a number of years ago, it was stocked with bass and various pan fish. Those fish have survived and thrived with very little human intervention. Despite Michigan's frigid winters and warm, muggy summers, they flourish. The environment seems to suit them rather well.

If you enjoy fishing and have kids, as I do, there is nothing much better than having a pond stocked with fish right in your front yard. And if the fish are bass and pan fish, that's just icing on the cake. Why, you ask? Let's just say intelligence is not among those species' strengths, especially for the pan fish. Put another way, if those species were the only ones people fished for, there would be no need for fish stories. The only thing difficult about catching those fish is making sure they don't swallow your hook.

I get a kick out of fishing with my kids in our pond. On such occasions I rarely get to drop my line in the water, partly because I spend a good deal of time untangling my kids' lines, putting worms on hooks, and making sure fish are the only creatures being hooked. (If you ever want a random body piercing, I invite you to join us for an afternoon of fishing.) Another reason I don't fish in our pond much is that bobber fishing with a worm holds little appeal for me. It's not that bobber fishing is beneath me: Catching fish is always better than not catching fish. But, with that said, I like challenges, and for me fly-fishing is a more inviting challenge.

I don't fly-fish for just any old species. Some of my younger years were spent in the Pacific Northwest, where the fish of choice is trout. For me, it was rainbow trout. I fondly remember warm summer days when my mom would take me to a creek near our home and I would spend hours hunting rainbows. They are not easy fish to catch, especially for a 10-year-old. They are smart and wary, challenging the angler to think about how to approach them, how to present the bait. Needless to say, hooking a big rainbow was one of the more exciting things I had done up to that point in my life.

While rainbows can be difficult to catch, when you get one on your line, that's an appropriate reward for a plan well executed. Just watching a rainbow jump out of the water flashing its namesake range of colors is a beautiful thing. So, I have an affinity for rainbow trout, something I want to pass down to my kids.

That's why I decided to plant some rainbows in our pond. I wanted my kids to have the experience of delicately placing a fly in front of a feeding trout and then waiting for the water's surface to break as the fish sucked in the bait. The fight afterward is great, but it's the presentation and anticipation of a "hit" that makes fly-fishing a great sport. I began the search for a trout farm where I could get some of these beautiful fish. It wasn't easy, but I finally succeeded. Excited, I called the place.

"Stoney Creek, may I help you?" an enthusiastic young woman answered. I asked if I could speak with someone about obtaining some rainbow trout. "I'll get my dad," she said.

After a few minutes I heard, "Yes, this is Steve. I hear you need some information about our trout."

I told Steve that I wanted to plant some rainbows in our pond, and he promptly asked me a number of questions regarding the size of the pond, its water source, what types of fish were already in it, and so on. I answered as best I could: "a half-acre...underground spring...bass and pan fish."

"Hmmm," Steve responded. "Do you know the temperature of the water?"

"It gets into the 70s during the summer."

Again Steve responded with, "Hmmm." Some type of language he had picked up from being around fish all day, I surmised. "I don't think the environmental conditions as you've described them are well suited for rainbows."

"Why's that?"

"Rainbows need highly oxygenated, cool water, ideally between 55 and 65 degrees. They can survive at slightly warmer temperatures, but it puts a lot of stress on them."

"So you don't think I can put rainbows in our pond?" I asked, obviously disappointed.

"If you do a few things to get more oxygen in the water and put some big logs into the pond to give the trout some shade, they will have a good chance of surviving. All you can do is try." He added that those changes also would benefit the bass and pan fish already in the pond—a point I didn't consider seriously at the time. With renewed excitement, I asked if he had the equipment I needed to oxygenate the pond, and he said he had aerators that would do the trick. The logs would be a cinch—we had a number of fallen trees on our property. I then asked Steve how many trout I should get and what size they should be. Steve asked me how big the bass in the pond were.

"The largest one I've caught was 18 inches," I said.

"Hmmm." The fish talk again.

With cautious optimism I queried, "What's the problem?"

"No problem," he said. "Just that you'll have to get some big trout. Bass can eat fish nearly as big as they are, or at least they'll try. If you don't get the right size trout, they won't have much of a chance in a small pond like yours. You'll need 10- to 12-inch trout to be safe. About 25 to 30 of them will do."

A few days later I drove out to Steve's farm and picked up the trout and the aerator. Steve reiterated the importance of setting up the aerator promptly and getting the logs in the water, not only for shade but also to provide some cover and safety for the trout. He was concerned that relocating the trout would make them weak and vulnerable to the bass, so they would need places to hide. I told him I would get everything set up pronto.

I brought the trout home and, with kid-like eagerness, released them in the water. They all survived the trip and, after getting their bearings, swam off into the deeper parts of the pond. I then began to set up the aerator, but it was getting dark and a refreshing evening rain had begun. I told myself I would get to the aerator and the logs the next day.

Well, I got busy. The "next day" turned into "next week," which turned into "next month." As time passed, I noticed signs that something was wrong. After putting the rainbows in the pond, I often watched for rings of water gently disturbing the pond's serene surface, signaling that the trout were rising to the top to feed. Initially, I observed frequent flurries of surface-breaking activity in the morning and evening hours as the trout rose to grab their bug-filled breakfasts and dinners. But over time the telltale rings, the observable indicators of trout life, gradually faded. By the time I put the aerator and logs into the pond, it was too late.

In their own way, the trout had been telling me they were struggling in their new home. But I didn't listen or pay attention. I assumed that, since they are considered to be strong fish, the rainbows would be okay until I had time to create the environment that would give them the best chance for survival. I waited too long, and the trout paid the price.

I learned a valuable lesson about having the right environment when planting trout. No matter how strong and healthy the fish were when I put them in the pond, unless I was willing to change the environment, taking their needs into consideration, I was doomed to lose them. The lesson was an expensive one: Big rainbow trout aren't cheap.

What's in Your Pond?

People are much the same as rainbow trout when it comes to their environment. We put a lot of stress on people when we don't develop an environment for them in which they can survive and, ultimately, thrive. The emotional, cognitive, and physical energy it takes to cope with an unfriendly and intolerant environment will drain even the best and brightest of their potential. The stress will eventually take its toll in the form of inefficiency, poor performance, absenteeism, and even declining health.

In the same way that I didn't take responsibility for the newcomers to our pond, many organizations don't provide for the needs of new employees. Worse, they blame the people themselves for their inability to thrive in an environment that's not conducive to their even *surviving*. Organizations often blame people for problems that have their roots in structures, systems, and scripts. Situational, organizational factors depriving "new fish" of a healthy workplace are commonly seen as dispositional, individual traits. That is, problems are seen to lie with the individual. And when individuals are seen as the "problem," usually little effort is made to uncover systemic issues of exclusion, inequity, and intolerance.

Just as there are real and meaningful differences between various species of fish and the environments they need, there are real and meaningful differences between people and their workplace requirements. Whether the differences are between people of color and white folks, between Baby Boomers and members of Generation Y, or between men and women, failure to develop an open-minded and respectful organization that takes people's needs into account makes us less efficient and hampers our ability to compete with organizations that have created truly inclusive and conducive environments.

Like me with the knowledge I gained from trout farmer Steve, some organizations do their homework and become aware of the meaningful differences between people. They become enlightened about what it means and what it takes to be truly diverse and inclusive. But, also like me, some don't do anything with that knowledge. These organizations conceptually understand the need to change their environment or culture, but they feel no urgency or motivating passion to do so. Important knowledge is not activated. Strategy is not executed.

Often, there is an underlying belief that the existing environment should be adequate for anyone because it suits the majority of people already there relatively well. But evidence points to the contrary. Indeed, differences do matter. And those organizations that understand this fundamental concept will be the most competitive in the future in terms of recruiting, hiring, and retaining the "best and brightest" candidates, a pool that demographers say is only growing more diverse.

If I were to do it again, I would put the aerator and logs in the pond well before I put in the trout. The pond would be prepared before the trout arrived, ensuring their best chance of survival. It really wouldn't have taken much effort on my part to develop an environment in which trout could thrive. If I had done what I knew I needed to do, my family and I would now have the benefit and thrill of catching rainbows right in our front yard. And as trout farmer Steve said to me, if I had taken the steps to make the environment good for the trout, I also would have made it better for the bass and pan fish. Doing right for some actually can make things better for all. Wow, what a great concept! An inclusive environment that respects the many, as well as the few, is the hallmark of successful organizations in the twenty-first century.

Improving the Pond's Environment

To help you start improving the water in your organization's pond, here are some questions to ask, an activity, and an assignment for this week.

1. **First glance.** Historically, who has survived and flourished in your organizational "pond"? What steps have been taken to develop an environment conducive to the survival of all "fish"?

2. **Looking inward.** What is your own experience in the pond? Are you flourishing or barely surviving? What about the environment needs to change for you to thrive? For others to thrive?

3. **What if?** What if the next generation of employees contains new species of fish? How will you make sure your pond is ready?

4. **Activity.** Ask participants to assess the water quality of your pond by identifying five or six cultural characteristics of the organization and how they contribute to a healthy or unhealthy environment. What new fish might be entering your pond soon? What conditions are necessary for them and the existing fish to flourish? Work together to identify the elements needed for your new and improved organizational pond. Determine action steps needed to create the type of pond environment in which everyone can flourish. And then do them!

5. **This week's assignment.** Identify one deficit in your organizational pond that *you* can begin addressing immediately.

| 2 |

A Better Script

Recently, I learned a lesson about how different perspectives and experiences produce different ways of seeing problems and, ultimately, different solutions to those problems. It's an embarrassing story, but I feel compelled to tell you about the power of "cognitive scripts."

The story begins with me being named the CVO ("Chief Vacuuming Officer") of my house, an honor bestowed by my wife. As CVO I report directly to the CEO (my wife) and I am responsible for vacuuming our house every week…or so. Yes, indeed, I am in charge of sucking dust!

I gave myself a nice budget for a vacuum cleaner and promptly spent it on the best money could buy. This is no ordinary vacuum cleaner. It has six wheels that all swivel for great maneuverability. Its 6-amp motor has sucking power akin to that of distant relatives of a new lottery winner. If you want a hose attachment, any hose attachment, this vacuum cleaner has it. It has lights to tell you when an area is clean or dirty. And talk about technology: It has this HEPA filter thing that the manufacturer claims will trap 99.9998 percent of all harmful particles. So you get the picture. I bought a twenty-fourth-century machine to wreak havoc on twenty-first-century dirt!

One day while vacuuming with this technological marvel, I heard a pop and suddenly felt air blowing on my leg. I looked down to see that the door holding the HEPA filter had popped open. Not a problem, I thought, as I closed the filter door and resumed my duties. Not long after, however, the door flew open again. I turned off the vacuum cleaner to take a closer look and noticed something wrong with the latch. It didn't seem like a big deal, so I tried one more time to see if the door might hold against the pressure of the vacuum. It did not. The latch was broken. And as I thought the word *broken*, a little script activated in my head and the word *tape* emerged.

At this point I need to let you in on a bit of my history. I am a tape man. That is, if something is broken, I use tape to fix it. It could be any kind of tape—Scotch, electrical, masking, or the Holy Grail of tapes… DUCT TAPE. Where did I learn this? Where did I get this "script"? Well, my stepfather taught me to use tape when I was a young boy. When things were broken, his solution was tape. He used tape to repair the torn wings of my paper airplanes, to hem his pants, and to seal leaky air hoses in our car. Tape wasn't messy and, more important, it always seemed to work.

So, to fix my vacuum cleaner, I retrieved some masking tape from our desk, placed a strip on the filter door, and then turned on the vacuum. I waited several minutes to see if the door would stay shut. And it did, as I knew it would. Fixed!

As I maneuvered the vacuum cleaner through the rooms on our main floor, I pondered the healing qualities of tape. Deep in thought and a little distraught about why tape has not received the credit it deserves, I again felt air blowing on my leg. The filter door had swung open again. Needs more tape, I thought.

I strategically placed more strips of masking tape until the filter door resembled a little cocoon. Surely this would hold. I began to vacuum again, but five minutes later the door flew open. Now I was getting frustrated. Obviously, I needed more tape. Not more quantity, more *quality*. Yes, I needed duct tape! With the roll in hand, using great care, I cut off a small piece, stuck it to my hand, and made my way back to the vacuum cleaner.

At about this time, my wife appeared, curious about why the vacuum cleaner was being turned on and off so often. She asked what was going on with the duct tape on my hand. As I explained about the filter door, she gave me that look that wives can give their husbands. You know, the one that says, "You're just stupid, aren't you?"

Without a word, but with a shake of her head, she walked over to the desk. At first I thought she was reaching for some tape, but her hand emerged holding a little rubber band. "Crazy woman," I thought. But I tried her solution because, after all, she is the CEO. I resumed vacuuming the carpet, certain that the dainty little rubber band soon would break. Secretly, I wanted the door to fly open, but five minutes went by, and then 10. The door remained shut. The rubber band was working. "Please break," I prayed to the tape gods. But the rubber band did not break.

I finished vacuuming and the rubber band held. Could it be that rubber bands are superior to tape? Now my simple tape-as-a-solution-to-everything-broken world was falling apart. From now on, I no longer could think only about tape, I would have to also think about rubber bands. As my synapses worked to reroute themselves, I came to understand that I had just been taught, or actually retaught, a valuable lesson.

So what had I learned? I "learned" what I have been telling others for years—that different people with different experiences often come up with different solutions. In this case, my paradigm for fixing things revolved around tape. But in this instance, tape didn't work. I spent at least 30 minutes trying to get tape to work, with no thought of seeking a different solution. Then my wife fixed the problem in a matter of seconds with her solution, a rubber band. I know that my ultimate solution, duct tape, would have worked. Everyone knows that, right? The filter door would have stayed shut with just a small piece of duct tape, but while the solution would have worked, it would not have been as elegant as a rubber band because duct tape always leaves some residue behind after you take it off.

I'm sure tape will always pop into my head as a first solution. However, it's likely that I will not have to stretch (pun intended) too far to come up with a rubber band as a viable alternative. Who knows, I might even extend beyond tape and rubber bands, on my own, willingly.

Can You Stretch Beyond Current Scripts?

There's nothing necessarily wrong with letting past experiences guide present actions. That's natural. But knowing that past experiences may not yield effective solutions to current problems should make us open to myriad diverse experiences—experiences that will give us new options the next time we face a problem. Along those lines, it's probably a good thing to have people around us whose experiences are different from ours. The more we surround ourselves with diverse perspectives, the greater the likelihood that we'll arrive at solutions we could not find based only on our own experiences.

Put simply, inclusion and diversity are naturally linked to creativity and innovation. Without the former, the latter doesn't exist.

Diversity of experiences, thoughts, and perspectives is the foundation for maximizing creativity and innovation. If we don't invite and include different ways of viewing problems and situations (and people with an open-minded approach to new ideas and perspectives), we stifle diverse thought (read: creativity and innovation).

Now the question becomes, "Are creativity and innovation important to your organization?" If not, from a business perspective there's not much need to work on issues of inclusion and diversity. But if new ideas and approaches are crucial to becoming "better, stronger, and faster" and staying ahead of the competition in a global environment, then the work of inclusion and diversity is not an option: It is an imperative.

As we continue the transition to a creative age fueled by ideas, the importance of creativity and innovation will only increase. Today, ideas matter. Tomorrow, ideas will matter more. In fact, one might say, "Ideas rule!" Are you limiting your organization's ability to generate novel ideas by limiting your diversity? Likewise, are you limiting the strength of the diversity you have by asking for sameness and assimilation or by requiring uniformity in the search for unity? If you don't find ways to genuinely include, value, and engage employees and allow their unique contributions, you are smothering the next breakthrough innovation.

I must confess that it will take some time and work on my part for tape to lose its position as the premier solution to all things broken. Some ideas just get stuck in our head. Developing an inclusion and diversity mind-set is hard work, but it's necessary if we are to operate smoothly in an increasingly diverse world where ideas matter, where creativity and innovation are the lifeblood of great organizations and of those that will be around for a long time, where limited thinking guarantees ultimate failure. If failure is not an option for you and your enterprise, then neither should be the work of inclusion and diversity.

Using Rubber Bands

To help you open your organization to new and different ideas and perspectives, here are some questions to ask, an activity, and an assignment for this week.

1. **First glance.** What are your organization's "broken = tape" scripts (that is, what are its historical approaches to problem solving)? Do the same people often propose these ideas? When was the last time a "rubber band" idea (i.e., a novel approach) was introduced, and who introduced it? How, and from where, did it arise?

2. **Looking inward.** What types of tape-only scripts run through your head as you face hurdles? Are you able to recognize the scripts and also grant yourself the freedom to entertain rubber band ideas?

3. **What if?** What would happen if your organization invited staff to suggest rubber band solutions to a problem? What if you found that rubber bands are just as strong as (or stronger than) tape?

4. **Activity.** A practical way to approach this concept is to break participants into groups of five or six, giving each person a sheet of paper. Ask each individual to write a real or hypothetical problem—one to which he or she needs a solution—at the top of the sheet. Now, pass the sheets around within each group. Have each participant write a solution to the problem posed at the top of each sheet. After everyone has had an opportunity to write on each of the sheets in his

or her group, return the sheets to their owners. Without considering whether the proposed solutions are good or bad, feasible or not, discuss what you have discovered. Highlight solutions that are rubber band ideas. Discuss ways to incorporate these in your workplace. Was there value in getting ideas from others in the group? What additional benefits (morale, employee buy-in on an idea, employee satisfaction from contributing to the project, and so on) could result from entertaining these ideas?

5. **This week's assignment.** Put away your tape and invite a colleague who isn't part of your usual team to supply some rubber bands.

| 3 |
Root Cause

Come spring in Michigan, I am busy scheming about the new golf equipment I will purchase for the upcoming golf season. By scheming, I mean formulating plans to convince my wife that a new set of shiny golf clubs glittering with the promise of lower scores are the key to my summer happiness. No matter that I bought new clubs the previous year, and the year before that, and the year before that—each new season requires the purchase of new clubs. The annual purchase of new golf equipment is the centerpiece of my strategy for getting better at golf. It's been my philosophy since my entrée into golf.

A little background; I didn't pick up golf until my late 20s. Oh yes, I had played a round here and there growing up, but as I crossed the bridge into my 30s, I felt the need to find a sport that I could play well into my later years. Golf seemed to fit the bill. By all appearances golf did not seem to be an activity that required a particularly fit body. Evidence of this comes from relatively good tour professionals with the nicknames of "The Walrus" and "Dumpy"—nicknames derived from the physical build of their bodies. While I still retained the competitiveness cultivated during a sports-filled childhood, the physical attributes necessary to be as competitive as my mind thought I could be had already begun their exodus. My left knee had given its two-week notice years ago, and shortly after, my right shoulder took advantage of an early retirement offer. My body was eager for the more comfortable and less painful movements required to navigate an electric golf cart with a drink in hand.

With my late start in golf, I felt an urgency to improve quickly. Hence my strategy for purchasing new equipment every year. What could go wrong? Golf equipment manufacturers are continually innovating. They assure that each new line of clubs, which so happen to come out every year, will help club owners hit the ball straighter, further, and with pinpoint accuracy. I know I shouldn't put full trust into their claims. They're just out to make a profit. And I don't. I psychologically reduce their claims by 10 percent and never pay retail prices. Okay, sometimes.

In the first year of employing my strategy, I improved relatively quickly. Obviously, the strategy had worked. The following year I purchased more new equipment. Again, I improved. It was in year three that I got more serious about golf, which meant serious golf purchases. No more knockoffs, just name brands. Deep into year three, I had what's called a "+9 handicap index." For you nongolfers out there, lower is better. Having a single digit index is good. Double digits, not so much. My improvement continued over the years to a +5 index. Zoom to the present, however, and my initial forward progress has stalled. In fact, if I look at my golf handicap index over the last five years, I've gotten worse. My index is now double digits. Notice that I have not provided those digits for you.

Here's what's interesting: in these last five years that my golf game degraded, I was still using my strategy of purchasing new equipment every year, the same strategy that helped me improve quickly in the early stages. Why is my strategy no longer working? Simply put, because equipment is no longer my problem. New equipment did all it could do for me. I venture to say the issue has more to do with not enough quality practice time. With that in mind let me offer this thought... *When you address the wrong issue, you rarely arrive at solutions for the real problem.* For engineers reading this, what likely popped into their heads is "root cause analysis." Indeed, I've been addressing the wrong issue for the last five years. I continued the pattern of purchasing new equipment every year, which had worked early on, but I was not putting in the time for deliberate and purposeful practice. I should have had no expectation of improving, or even staying at the same skill level, if I am not addressing the "root cause" of my downhill slide.

With the idea of "root cause" in mind, let me now offer this hypothesis as it relates to the work of inclusion and diversity... *Diversity is not the problem. It's closed-mindedness.* If this is true, then many, with good intentions, have been putting time and resources into the wrong place as they address issues of inclusion and diversity. If the root cause of so-called "diversity problems" is, in large part, closed-mindedness, then we must have a paradigm shift in how we think about issues of inclusion and diversity and how we address such issues. Let's examine this a little closer to better understand why closed- or narrow-mindedness might be the real issue in need of addressing.

Imagine you have a room full of people representing all kinds of human "diversity," meaning different races, genders, educational backgrounds, personalities, professions, etc. Now, let's make these people closed-minded. What might you get? Well, that sounds a lot like the United States Congress! Okay, more seriously, **Diversity + Closed-mindedness** is a great recipe if you're cooking up a dish of misunderstanding, miscommunication, and conflict. It does not take much imagination to see how an inability or unwillingness to listen to and work with those who are different than you can lead to these and other negative outcomes.

Now, make a slight change to the equation. Keep the exact same diversity but make the people in the room more open-minded and curious, people who put effort into listening to others who are different with the goal of understanding. Make these people more willing to step out of their comfort zones, ones who enjoy entertaining new ideas and are better able to "agree to disagree." With that change you fundamentally change the potential of the group for realizing more positive outcomes like better collaboration, more opportunities, greater creativity and innovation, etc.! Indeed, **Diversity + Open-mindedness** yields very different outcomes than **Diversity + Closed-mindedness**. And keep in mind, the diversity in the room has not changed. The only things that've changed are the people's mind-set, attitude, and appreciation of human differences; in short, of diversity.

If we want to understand the previous ideas in terms of inclusion and exclusion, consider these two general equations:

Diversity + Open-mindedness = Inclusion
Diversity + Closed-mindedness = Exclusion

Human diversity is potentially a powerful asset. We, both individuals and organizations, waste that asset when closed-mindedness prevails. Alternatively, the power of human differences is leveraged and unleashed when more of us can be open-minded. A great benefit of appreciating closed-mindedness as the root problem rather than diversity is that we all, as individuals, can work on becoming more curious and open-minded. We do not have to wait for leaders on high to set up a program or initiative (though one can be helpful). And open-mindedness can aid us in many areas of our lives if one considers that open-mindedness is required for learning, for improving.

Speaking of improving, I have made a commitment to taking my golf game to another, better level. I will redirect my resources from buying new golf equipment to getting some golf lessons. I'll do my best to be open to the swing changes the teacher will invariable ask me to make. I plan on practicing and playing more. With a better understanding of what my root problem is, I am in a better position to return to single-digit handicap status. Unfortunately, I made this commitment after ordering a new set of clubs.

Examining Root Cause

To help you consider going beyond the superficial and what's easily seen, here are some questions to ask, an activity, and an assignment for this week.

1. **First glance.** Share your reaction to the idea that "diversity is not the problem, it's closed-mindedness."

2. **Looking inward.** How has closed-mindedness impacted you and your understanding of people and ideas that are "different"?

3. **What if?** What if you and your organization started practicing open-mindedness? What would that look like?

4. **Activity.** In a small group, discuss how a greater curiosity and open-mindedness could help your organization.

5. **This week's assignment.** Think about some ways you can personally practice curiosity and open-mindedness. What would they look like? Now, go practice.

| 4 |

Equal Is Not Always Fair

A few years ago I attended a conference at a hotel in one of my favorite cities, Chicago. After checking in and finding my room I, like always, explored the venue. As I walked the halls looking for the fitness area (healthy living always begins with good intentions) and busily checking voicemail with my cell phone, I entered what I thought was the men's restroom. I immediately noticed something wrong: I could find no urinals on the wall. There were five stalls but no urinals. And the clinching telltale sign: This place I thought was the men's room smelled rather nice—as I imagined a women's restroom would.

Immediately realizing that this was not where I should be, I left. Fortunately, no one observed my absent-minded, cell-phone-enabled mistake.

I went across the hall to the men's restroom and, comforted by the urinals, did what I set out to do. On my way out, I noticed that there were three urinals and two stalls. The architects who designed these buildings must be enlightened about gender equality, I thought, comparing the five places for relief in the women's restroom and the five places in the men's restroom. Feeling good about the state of gender equality regarding restrooms, I retired to my room for a good night's rest.

The conference began the next day with a great opening session during which everyone seemed to have a cup, or two or three, of coffee or tea. At break time, there was the expected rush of people in search of restrooms. Some people fired up their cell phones as they searched. Big mistake, I thought.

I, too, had to use the restroom, and I knew exactly where it was. As I approached the men's room, I looked across the hall. A long line had formed at the entrance to the women's restroom. I then looked to where I was headed. There was no line, and no wait, at my restroom. Yes!

Feeling a little guilty about my immediate relief, I thought about what I had observed. Long line for women. No line for men. Hmmm. This might not be fair, my inner voice of justice and fairness whispered.

I thought about the building's architects and my recent sense of satisfaction with restroom equality. The architects, most likely male, had done the "equal" thing. Five relief places for women, five relief places for men. Conceptually, it seems like the right thing to do.

But the break in the conference exposed a different operational reality. Treating people equally is not necessarily the same as treating people fairly. Without going into too much detail, let's just say that men require less time to use the bathroom, on average, than do women. Hence, longer lines for women.

And that's only the physical aspect of going to the bathroom. There are other differences. While I have not done any scientific study, my informal observations suggest that women are more likely to use a bathroom trip as a mini social outing. I have often observed women inviting

26

other women to the restroom, but I have not personally heard one man say to another man, "Hey, come with me to the bathroom. I need to talk to you about something." So the women's room lines are longer because there are also more individuals in them.

What's Your Corporate Blueprint?

It's often easier to treat people equally than to treat them fairly. Applying the concept of equal treatment to restrooms, for example, requires little thought. One makes a rule (five relief places for each gender) and applies it without giving much consideration to differences that may be found in the subjects to which the rule is being applied. But is it fair if people are substantively different?

The very fact that the application of an "equal treatment" policy produces different outcomes among different groups should trigger further inquiry and questioning. Note that I did not say that an equal treatment policy is always wrong. What I am saying is that it is not always right in a world filled with myriad types of people representing multiple belief systems and ways of doing things. If we live in a truly diverse world, then "equal treatment" approaches must always be examined through the lens of fairness.

If my example of how real biological and sociological differences between men and women can affect going to the restroom did not convince you, consider this question: What if there were a policy to promote only people with good leadership qualities (not necessarily a bad policy) *and* men (because they have historically held positions of leadership and thus got to write books on leadership) get to define what those qualities are (qualities often based on how they were raised and on male-oriented societal expectations of what it means to be a man)? Put differently, what might happen if a male-created mental model of how a leader should look and act looks and acts like a man? Might it contribute to the fact that, in 2008, 488 of the Fortune 500 CEOs were men? That's 97.6 percent of all the Fortune 500 CEOs. From a "glass half-full" perspective, that is a couple of percentage points better than it was a couple of hundred years ago, when 100 percent of the most powerful positions in the fledgling country were held by men. Hooray for progress! From another perspective, such "progress" is unjust, unfair, and inequitable.

Fair as opposed to equal treatment entails more analysis and examination, maybe more research and consideration. It usually involves more time and more thinking. And it's likely to require a different type of thinking, with different thinkers with different perspectives around the table. If you are passionate about justice, then give the concept of fairness a fair chance.

Adding More Stalls

Might some of your organization's policies, behaviors, and practices negatively (or positively) affect certain groups more than others? To help you examine that possibility, here are some questions to ask, an activity, and an assignment for this week.

1. **First glance.** What are some examples of "equal but not fair" in your organization? What leadership qualities are promoted in your organization?

2. **Looking inward.** Think about a time when you were treated equally but not fairly. What would a more fair treatment have been?

3. **What if?** What if your organizational blueprint is more "fair" for some than for others? What new "architects" might you need to assist with your redesign?

4. **Activity.** In a group, brainstorm some other examples of when equal may not be fair. If you find this difficult, ask if there are any left-handed people in the group. Ask them if it was *equal* and *fair* when their grade school teachers passed out right-handed scissors to the entire class. Ask them if it is *fair* that most power tools today are designed for a right-handed world. What would the equal response be? What would the fair response be?

5. **This week's assignment.** Think fairly—and act with a "fairness" orientation. Practice fair treatment by considering the many ways people may be different or may be dealing with different circumstances.

| 5 |

It's All in the Details

When my eldest son was just 18 months old he had two canine encounters that affect him to this day. The first came on a nice spring day while he was in our backyard. As my son was playing with his assortment of toy cars and trucks, the neighbor's dog came running over. Before I could react, the little dog lovingly "attacked" my son, licking his face, jumping on him, and knocking him down. That's something that excited, playful dogs do, and this dog meant no harm. But, as you can imagine, my son was quickly in tears.

Shortly after that incident, my son encountered a much bigger dog at a local park. This dog, a good-sized German shepherd, wandered in from nearby during our picnic and attempted to snatch a slice of pizza from my son's hands. At first my son held on tightly, unwilling to give up his lunch. The dog, as stubborn, let my son know who the eventual winner would be by producing a menacing growl. My son quickly let go and in the process fell down, hurting his behind. Again, the tears flowed.

Whether it was the incident in the park or the combination of the

31

two tear-filled encounters I do not know, but from that point on my son was deathly afraid of *all* dogs. No matter their size or their demeanor or what they are doing, in my son's mind dogs are something to be feared. A dog could be the nicest canine in the world, but my son will not go near it.

Interestingly, my son can watch his three younger siblings play with a dog, and still he won't approach it. He can see that the dog isn't harming his brothers and sister, but that isn't proof that the dog will be equally harmless to him. I thought he would outgrow the fear he had as a toddler, but it is as strong today as it was then.

On one level, I can't understand my son's fear of every dog he sees, especially when there is observable evidence that a particular dog is not dangerous. On a different level, my inability to understand is clear. The problem I have in understanding my son's fear is that I am looking at it from my perspective. It's easy for me not to be afraid of dogs because I've never had a bad encounter with a dog. I know that some dogs can be mean and dangerous. I also know that many are playful and harmless. The reality in which I dwell leads me to examine clues that might distinguish a potentially threatening dog from a playful one. My son's reality does not include that type of examination.

If I tried to understand my son's fear of dogs without taking into consideration his two encounters with dogs when he was young, I might label his fear irrational, baseless, and incomprehensible. I might even say he's being "too sensitive." But by taking those "details" into account, I gain a greater appreciation and understanding of why he clings to my leg when a dog approaches.

By validating his fear as rational and understandable, I give myself patience to figure out creative approaches to, and ultimately solutions for, his fear of dogs. More important, though, when I validate his fear, I validate his reality. I am telling him that his reality is just as valid as mine. Ultimately I am validating him as a human being who not only *deserves* respect and understanding but also *should receive* respect and understanding. There is a difference between deserving and receiving.

Whose Shoes Are You Wearing?

Many of us have difficulty understanding the actions of others because we evaluate those actions against the backdrop of what we think we would do in the same situation. We believe the shoes we are walking in are the other person's shoes—but they are actually our own. Put another way, when we make attributions and judgments about the behaviors of others based on our limited experiences and knowledge, we are prone to make mistakes. Why? Because we fill in the gaps in our knowledge with information that comes straight out of our own reality, our own world, our own belief system. I call this being "empa-centric" rather than empathetic.

Empathy has to do with being able to identify with another's thoughts, feelings, and attitudes. Being genuinely empathetic requires us to have knowledge about others—their history, their reality, their world. Without adequate knowledge we are to some degree guessing what it would be like to be in their situation—and we are apt to be empa-centric. An empa-centric person, who may sincerely desire to be empathetic, brings along all of his or her personal assets in answering the question, "What would I do in their shoes?"

We saw a prime example of this following Hurricane Katrina in 2005. I'm sure you heard or read accounts of people—who lived nowhere near New Orleans—saying things like, "If I knew the hurricane was coming days in advance, I would have gotten out of there." Those people were unable to identify with what it would be like to not have bus fare—or even a bus to use it on. They incorporated their reality into the decision making. I'm sure some were imagining themselves driving out of New Orleans in their new Lexus!

No doubt you've been privy to conversations in which someone has said, "I'd never talk to the boss like that," or, "What would possess someone to get upset about that promotion? Harry's been in line for that job for years." When we mentally re-create the situation to determine our response, we sometimes leave out important details that likely would influence our actions in the same circumstances. We tend to be empa-centric when trying to walk in the shoes of others, especially when those others are very different from us. So often we can't even get out of our own shoes!

No wonder it's hard for many white people to understand and accept it when people of color bring up race as a recurring issue. If one never experiences what it's like being nonwhite in a white-dominated workforce and/or doesn't know much about the country's racial history, it's easy to dismiss affirmative action policies as unfair and unnecessary, and to make accusations of using the "race card."

If someone isn't homosexual or has no gay or lesbian friends, it can be difficult for him or her to accept the idea that homosexuality may not be a choice or to understand how painful it can be to live out one's life in a culture and world that are designed for heterosexuals and that often punish those who are "other than."

If someone is not a woman, it is harder to understand how those "harmless" jokes told in the workplace contribute to a glass ceiling in many organizations, or how the networking and relationship-building ritual of playing golf can serve to include some and exclude many others.

If someone is part of the dominant culture and benefits from the status quo, it is easier to label attempts to produce greater fairness, justice, and equity as acts of "political correctness."

So the next time you catch yourself saying or thinking something like, "It's nothing, quit being so sensitive," or, "Why do you have to see it that way?" ask yourself if you've taken enough details into account. And ask yourself whether those types of comments and questions come from an empathetic heart or an empa-centric one. The former cares. The latter blames.

Changing Shoes

To help you encourage people in your organization to step into someone else's shoes, here are some questions to ask, an activity, and an assignment for this week.

1. **First glance.** Consider any instances of conflict in your organization. Was the conflict caused even in part by misunderstandings or differences in viewpoint? What happened?

2. **Looking inward.** Focusing on one particular issue, describe your "shoes"—your collection of experiences and knowledge that make you who you are today. Now imagine for a moment that you are changing out of your shoes and into someone else's. What information are you missing about the other person? What experiences, realities, and background are you bringing with you?

3. **What if?** What if your organization's leadership tried on each other's shoes? What if they tried on the shoes of those on a different level, in a different department?

4. **Activity.** In a group setting, discuss an article from the newspaper or a recent workplace policy change or conflict. Ask people to share their reactions and perspectives. Listen, reserve judgment, and then, as a group, explore these questions: How does hearing varied points of view reframe your understanding of the topic, your empathy for the situation? Are you able to see through another lens, or do you cling tightly to the lens you've always known?

5. **This week's assignment.** Expand your knowledge of those around you by "trading shoes" with another person. Remember to ask yourself whether you are truly putting on the other's shoes (being empathetic) or just putting your own shoes back on (being empa-centric).

| 6 |

Below the Surface

One of my brothers called me recently so we could start planning our annual fishing trip to Canada. It's a big family event that all five brothers await eagerly. Avid fishermen, we take the sport seriously, or as seriously as we can without people (i.e., our wives) calling us obsessive. Our wives find our attachment to rods and reels and artificial lure "bugs" just a little unnatural.

While our trip usually involves a hunt for walleye and pike, I've been pushing for a place to pull out my fly rod for some trout. Fly-fishing first caught my fancy when I saw the movie *A River Runs through It*. Critics gave the film a thumbs-up for its theme, story line, and lessons. I liked all the scenes of big trout being caught with bamboo fly rods. It was a glimpse of heaven to me, watching those boys whip figure eights with their fly lines and cast their bug-like bait with pinpoint accuracy. But what intrigued me most was watching the fly drift lazily on top of the water and then, without warning, get engulfed in a mighty splash. Now, that's fly-fishing. Or so I thought.

After watching the movie, I went to buy fly-fishing equipment at a local shop. When I walked into the store, I looked around in amazement at all the gear, enough to plunge the purchaser into poverty. As I loitered in a mix of awe and confusion, the store owner broke me out of my trance, saying, "Somethin' I can help you with?" I told him I had just seen *A River Runs through It* and wanted to get into fly-fishing. He gave a little laugh and queried further, "Do you want to really learn how to fly-fish or do you want to do it the way you saw it in the movie?"

I was stumped. I didn't know there was a difference. The owner began to explain, "What you saw in the movie is not how real fly-fishers fish."

"Real fly-fishers?" I mumbled.

"Yes, real fly-fishers are the ones who actually catch big fish on a consistent basis. They don't do that movie stuff."

"What do you mean, 'that movie stuff'?"

He continued, "In the movie all you saw were people fishing with what we call dry flies—flies that float on top of the water."

I interrupted, "Yeah. Isn't that fly-fishing—casting a fly, letting it float downstream, and waiting for a fish to come up and get it?"

"That's only a small part of fly-fishing. When you're fishing for trout, you have to understand that 90 percent of the time trout, especially the big ones, eat under the surface of the water. For example, trout generally grab nymphs as the nymphs are making their way to the surface. They rarely break the surface to eat. Most of the action takes place where you can't see it. In reality, the best fly-fishers use what we call wet flies and nymphs that don't float. To be an effective fly-fisher, you have to be keenly aware of what happens below the surface of the water."

As he finished his coaching session, I began to understand that what I believed to be the entirety of fly-fishing was only the small, "showy" part of this wonderful sport. Perhaps most people who don't know much about fly-fishing think about it the way I did—as surface action, easily seen.

Where Are You Fishing?

I suppose it is much the same way with issues of discrimination—racism, sexism, ageism, homophobia, and so on. Those who have not faced or witnessed much discrimination tend to recognize it only in obvious acts—the "surface action" easily recognized by most people. Those acts include cross burnings and crude, demeaning jokes directed at women in the workplace, for example, as well as words like *faggot* and *spic* written on the walls and mirrors of offices. This is obvious discrimination, the "dry flies" of prejudice and exclusion. But such acts make up only about 10 percent of all discriminatory behavior.

It's the remaining 90 percent of discrimination that should catch most of our attention. It's the below-the-surface, subtle activities that cause the most harm. Unfortunately, most of us can't, don't, or won't look below the surface to see what's happening. And often, when we are told what's happening below the surface, our reaction tends to be one of disbelief or amazement.

Most discriminatory behaviors, even our own acts, occur beneath the threshold of our daily awareness. Often, we see but don't recognize them. I call these "acts of unintentional intolerance." For those of us who fall into this category (I daresay that's all of us), our job is to put on the wet gear and dive below the surface to experience, engage, and encounter lives that have been, for the most part, outside our awareness. In doing so, we might begin to see a whole new world. It is a world that might cause us great dissonance at first, but one we will come to understand. And with understanding will come less fear, more comfort, and greater appreciation for all the things that make us unique—and all the things we have in common. Strangers will become less strange.

Where do you spend the majority of your time addressing issues of discrimination, inequality, and injustice? Is it with "surface action" issues that are easily seen but may not get at the root of the matter, or is it with the tougher, less obvious issues that aren't as splashy but offer greater rewards?

Observing Deeper

To help you encourage people in your organization to see the actions below the surface, here are some questions to ask, an activity, and an assignment for this week.

1. **First glance.** What are some examples of discriminatory behaviors that occur today at the surface level? What types of actions happen below the surface? What do you think the "fish" below are thinking as they watch us tackle the surface of discrimination?

2. **Looking inward.** Consider your behavior. Put on the "wet suit" and dive deeply into your activities and conversations. How can you engage lives and experiences that have been beneath your level of awareness?

3. **What if?** What if there are under-the-surface acts happening in your organization that are creating intolerance, bias, and prejudice? What steps are you taking to "fish more deeply" to identify them?

4. **Activity.** In a group, starting at the surface and working more deeply, describe some daily experiences or observations of discriminatory behaviors. This can be tough and uncomfortable, but it's necessary for the work of plunging below the surface. Listen to the stories shared in the group. What is happening below the surface that you didn't know before? Discuss what you as individuals can do to identify and change those behaviors.

Observing Deeper (cont'd)

5. **This week's assignment.** Go "deep-see" fishing (or out to lunch) with someone with whom you are not already comfortable. Listen, share, and acquire some new knowledge that you can take to a greater depth.

| 7 |

Lazy Brains

The sign on the treadmill read: "For the consideration of our other guests, please do not use this equipment for more than 45 minutes." I chuckled out loud as I wondered if this sign was truly necessary. How many people could this apply to? Let me be clear; the little notice taped onto the machine did not have a hyphen between the 4 and the 5, to mean "four to five minutes." No, it was telling the user to refrain from using the treadmill for more than three-quarters of an hour!

Okay, I admit it—I am lazy. But I have a perfectly valid reason—my brain makes me do it, or in this case, not do it. Recent advances in neuroscience suggest that the piece of gray-and-white matter between my ears is rather lazy. It tries to do the least amount of work possible. Put more positively, my brain (like all brains) works on an efficiency principle. That is, the human brain, as it works to help us navigate our world, is constantly trying to conserve energy.

To understand this a little better, it's good to know a few things about the brain. In the average human adult, the brain accounts for 2 to 3 percent of the body's mass but requires about 20 percent of the body's energy. For its size, the human brain uses a disproportionate amount of the body's energy. Varying estimates suggest that the energy consumed by the human brain at any given moment in time is enough to light up a 20- to 40-watt light bulb. And this is not fake or imaginary energy. It's energy in the form of glucose. Your brain runs in large part on sugar.

Consider this experience many have. You go to work, do nothing really physical all day, but come home completely exhausted. Yep, thinking requires energy. Processing information requires neurons and synapses to activate, which requires, you got it, glucose. It's not that each neuron or synapse requires much energy, it's that you have lots of them. The average adult human brain contains about 100 billion neurons with 10^{15} synaptic connections. Researchers estimate that there are more neurons and synapses in the human brain than there are stars and planets in our Milky Way galaxy.

An efficient human brain makes sense when viewed from an evolutionary perspective. In dangerous hostile environments where food was scarce, all else equal, the most efficient creatures survived! Efficiency is about energy conservation. The less energy you use during typical activities, the more energy you have on hand to deal with creatures that eye you as their own energy source, as well as other energy-draining aspects of your hostile surroundings. In Darwinian-based ancestral environments, inefficiency meant slow, and slow meant death. Most of us don't live in the same danger-filled conditions that our predecessors faced, but the brain still operates as if it were in a hostile environment. It still tries to conserve energy.

To the brain, time is energy, and one of the ways it conserves precious energy is to make decisions quickly. In order to accelerate decision making, our brain utilizes things called "mental models" and "mental maps," which are built from past experiences. We use these cognitive representations to make quick decisions, judgments, and evaluations. However, the ability to make quick decisions, judgments, and evaluations does not guarantee that we'll make good ones. The "goodness" of things like judgments and evaluations is highly dependent upon the data contained in our mental models and maps.

Now imagine making decisions and judgments using mental models and mental maps built on limited data, or worse, false data. Combine that with a brain that, as a means for conserving energy, has a great tendency to trade accuracy for speed and quality for quickness and you can you begin to see how this might possibly lead to inaccurate and sometimes flat-out false evaluations of people (and their ideas). Especially when those people are different from us, the strangers and outsiders with whom we may have little actual experience?

So, why might we have less experience with those we deem unlike us? Again, we can direct our attention to the brain's desire to conserve energy. When we encounter something different, something new and novel, we force more neurons and synapses to go *online*, and that requires more energy. From a cognitive science perspective, this is a strong explanation for why we like to stay in our comfort zones. Relatively fewer neural networks have to go online when we are not confronted with new and novel data. Outside the comfy confines of the familiar, we are forced to activate more and different sets of neural networks. Thus, more energy is spent.

The efficiency principle helps to explain why we hang out with people who think and believe as we do. It requires less energy, relatively speaking, to spend more of our time with like-minded people. Like-minded people by definition hold similar viewpoints, share common beliefs, and have perspectives in alignment. Moreover, if we hung out with people who differed in their beliefs and perspectives, we'd have to spend time and valuable energy explaining to these "outsiders" why they are wrong. Why bother when we can just surround ourselves with people who will tell us how right we are—folks who will affirm our current way of thinking and doing? Why expend more energy when the status quo is so comfortable and energy efficient?

The answer is greater creativity and innovation (i.e., better problem-solving abilities). Research clearly supports the idea that many different perspectives are better than a homogenous set of perspectives when it comes to problem solving. If past experiences directly impact our ability to identify problems and solutions, it logically follows that the more (and different) sets of past experiences and knowledge one has on hand, the greater the likelihood the most optimal solution will be found. It should then come as no surprise that the best lifeline to use when you are a contestant on the show *Who Wants to Be a Millionaire* is to ask the audience. The "Ask the Audience" lifeline is far better than the "Expert" lifeline. Based on data from this popular television game show, the audience has been correct 91 percent of the time. The expert, though good, is correct only 65 percent of the time (to understand the mathematical rigor behind this, read up on Bernoulli's Law of Large Numbers). The key is the diversity of experiences within the audience, and that each audience member's answer is included in the final calculation without group pressure to conform.

So there you have it. The power of inclusion and diversity is found in the audience's packaged ability to facilitate problem solving. We often don't leverage this power because our brains, in their quest to be as efficient as possible, prefer to exclude ideas, people, and things that are new, novel, and strange. They are stuck in the status quo. However, true innovation does not occur within comfortable quarters. It requires the spark that comes from the intersection of many perspectives, the collision of different domains of knowledge, and even the discomfort that arises from clashing viewpoints.

Picasso said, "The first step of creativity begins with the act of destruction." Could it be that destroying that which is familiar (current mental models and maps) by engaging with the unfamiliar is required for novel thinking and creative problem solving? If so, then we must be willing to challenge ourselves to venture beyond our comfort zones and into the comfort zones of others who view the world differently than we do. This won't be easy. Our brains will resist. They want to conserve energy, and leaving our comfort zones requires spending energy. But it can be done, and it must be done if we truly want to unleash the power of inclusion and reap the rewards of diversity.

"No pain, no gain," the saying goes. The next time I get on a treadmill, I'm going to push myself beyond 45 minutes. It will be uncomfortable, but I know there is much to be gained from spending that extra energy to break old routines. See you at the gym!

Work Out Your Brain

To help your brain get used to paying more attention to people and ideas that you might not be used to or familiar with, here are some questions to ask, an activity, and an assignment for this week.

1. **First glance.** How have your organizing skills been limited by your brain's desire to conserve energy? Discuss this question with respect to people and ways of doing.

2. **Looking inward.** With a critical eye, examine how your "lazy brain" may have placed limits on how you think, how you conduct your relationships, and how you live your day-to-day life.

3. **What if?** What if you practiced overcoming your brain's desire to conserve energy? What might happen if you decided to "encounter new and novel things" more often? How could that change your life in a positive manner?

4. **Activity.** In a small group, discuss examples of how "lazy brains" in the workplace have limited the growth of both individuals and their organization.

5. **This week's assignment.** Do something new and novel each day to work out your brain, to push it out of its comfort zone, and to show it that there are rewards for not being lazy. The more you practice, the easier it becomes to do.

| 8 |
Cool Features

Those who know me relatively well will agree with the statement that I am a lover of all things tech. I'm constantly in search of all things electronic with a sometimes-unquenchable desire to own the latest and greatest. I'm also a technology "early adopter," which means retailers of these glorious gadgets love me, and I'm not wise enough to wait several months for prices to go down and bugs to be fixed.

Moreover, I am an Apple fanatic (hear that, people at Apple?). I've had all things Apple ever since Mr. Jobs and Mr. Wozniak first put their products on the market. From the original Macintosh computer to the current Mac Pro, I have had enough Apple products to fill a football field. My favorite among Apple's offerings is the groundbreaking iPhone. Like Apple's computers, I've have had iPhones since they first popped onto the scene. When I was younger, I waited in long lines to purchase an iPhone. Even today, I am still an early adopter and want to be among the first to get a new iPhone, but now I wait in line online.

My current iPhone, the X, is a technological and artistic masterpiece.

A beauty to behold, it sports a 5.8-inch super-retina edge-to-edge display. Apple describes it as "the first OLED screen that rises to the standards of an iPhone, with accurate, stunning colors, true black, high brightness, and a 1,000,000 to 1 contract ratio." Yeah, it looks good! Its engine is an A11 Bionic chip with 64-bit architecture, neural engine, and embedded M11 motion coprocessor. It shoots video in 4k at 60 frames per second. I could tell you what all this means, but then I'd have to kill you. Trust me, this thing is cool. I can go online, watch movies, and purchase things, anything with a wave of my iPhone. With all the available apps I can do everything from tune my guitar to mindlessly practice mindfulness. I can run slide shows and store tens of thousands of songs and videos on it. It has face-recognition technology that allows me to unlock it with a quick glance. I believe it can also turn into a backyard barbeque and probably aid in Russian meddling. I have, however, been unable to find the apps for those particular transformations. Did I mention that this thing is cool?

The first time I pulled out my iPhone X on a plane, the people around me drooled in envy. I generally strive for humility, but this was too much. Just to rub it in, I lifted my iPhone X and looked at the screen and it magically turned on and unlocked. A little kid across the aisle nearly fell into unconsciousness with awe. But the show was not over. I then reached into a pocket of my backpack and pulled out a pleasantly designed white container. From it I withdrew a similarly cool pair of white, wireless Bluetooth AirPod headphones. They automatically sync with my iPhone X and turn on as I place them in my ears to listen to the Backstreet Boys. Yeah, I got it going on.

As with most of the features Apple's designers so brilliantly included in the X (that's how cool people refer to it), I rarely use them. I'm told my X can do lots of things that I don't know about. I primarily use my X to make calls, text my family, and keep my calendar. While I do go online with it, it's mostly it's to check sports scores and see what the weather will be like. I don't even illegally download music. I could, but I don't. What do I use my iPhone X for? Mostly I use it to remind me of things I should be doing, and to get the phone numbers for people who can help me with the things I should be doing. That's right, I use a $1,000 gadget for something a $10 paper-based planner can do. I do use the alarm clock feature, something my previous Franklin planner didn't have. So I really do feel better about spending all that money.

Could I be more efficient if I took advantage of all the iPhone's diverse features? Yes. Do I want to take the time and go through the hassle to learn about all those features? No. I think all those apps made for the iPhone are cool and could be useful, but I just can't seem to find the time to travel up the steep learning curve. I brag about the ability to do many things with my iPhone, but I have not come close to utilizing all its diverse features and take advantage of its multitude of capabilities—to help me get more work done, to be more efficient…to be better.

Do Some of Your Best Features Go Unused?

Thinking about how I fail to use all the diverse features of my iPhone X leads me to think about the many organizations that don't use all their talents and skills because they've branded people in some way—by race, gender, age, what department they work in and even by where they went to school. For example, a company might hire a talented marketer who happens to be Asian and then expect that person to develop marketing plans targeted only at Asian groups. That person may or may not be skilled at marketing to Asian groups, but limiting the job neglects ideas and solutions that might apply to marketing in many areas.

Many organizations place great value on what some call "male attributes," such as aggressiveness, competitiveness, and individuality. These companies may punish (intentionally and unintentionally) those who show so-called female attributes, such as cooperation, group orientation, and nurturing, because these are seen as weaknesses. An organization's inability to embrace the strengths found in its entire community will prevent it from taking advantage of opportunities that require different ways of viewing the world.

Taking steps to create a diverse workforce is one thing. Doing away with old structures and traditional methods so that a diverse workforce can excel is quite another. That is the heavy lifting of inclusion. It takes time and patience to transform traditional cultures into cultures that can take advantage of existing and potential talent, which will not necessarily be packaged in the expected, the familiar, or the comfortable. Organizations that work through the pain of transformation will unleash the power of inclusion and leverage the strength of diversity to its fullest.

I will be taking my own advice and learning more about how to use the many features of my iPhone X. It will take some time, but I am making a conscious effort to do so.

And did I mention that I just got the newest drone? It has a lot of cool features.

No Features Left Behind

Is it time to unpack your "iPhone?" To help you embrace all the "gadgets" in your organization, here are some questions to ask, an activity, and an assignment for this week.

1. **First glance.** What talents are underutilized in your organization? Is the organization stuck with focusing on just a few features? Who in your organization chooses which features will be valued?

2. **Looking inward.** What talents do you possess that are currently untapped? Have you been branded for a certain task and function? Have you taken conscious steps to utilize all of your "features" and those of the people around you?

3. **What if?** What if you are missing opportunities by underutilizing the talents of your gay employees, your black female employees, or others because you have pegged them for something else?

4. **Activity.** In a group, take turns sharing your talents—that's right, brag a little! Think about your areas of expertise, your talents, and your passions both in and outside the workplace. What features that are not being tapped does each person bring to the workplace? How might your organization go about learning of and using all the features in the group?

5. **This week's assignment.** Do a feature inventory of your organization, department, and/or coworkers, critically examining whose talents may not yet have been given the chance to activate.

| 9 |

A Difference in Weight

It was the start of a new year, and like a migrating goose I had made my annual return to our local health club. You know, to shed a few pounds and transform my average Hyundai body into a stunning BMW physique. No, really, I would.

My first trip back was invigorating, so to speak. There's nothing like the smell of a men's locker room to shock one out of the exercise doldrums. The aroma of sweaty towels spiced with athletic club–brand underarm spray brought back faint memories of my collegiate athletics days.

After leaving the locker room, I made my way to the stationary bikes for some cardio time. As I stood looking at the rows of bikes and bike-like machines, I marveled at human rationality. It takes a special kind of species to develop contraptions that require significant physical effort but in the end take the rider nowhere.

Oh, for the days when one could hop on a bike and start pedaling... and actually go somewhere. Yes, I know, I could still do that, but *you* try riding a bike in a snowy Michigan January. Plus, it's so uncool to travel real miles in the twenty-first century when one can navigate virtual miles.

I was feeling good about myself as I approached my goal of 30 minutes on the bike...29:57, 29:58, 29:59, 30:00! Done. As I stopped pedaling, I pressed the "Summary" button to reassure myself that there had been some result other than just the sweat flowing from my body and the pain pulsing through my legs. I wanted to know how many real calories I had burned. And there it was on the screen before me: I had ridden 4.7 electronic miles and worked off an amazing 150 calories. Wow! In the short span of 30 minutes, I had rid myself of the 12 ounces of Coke I had guzzled in 30 seconds at lunch. The reality of that input-output equation, though depressing, would not deter me from my fitness goals. I went off to the place where serious body sculptors go—the free weights area.

I initiated my weight work with some bench presses to rebuild my atrophying chest.

I started off with 45-pound plates, which, added to the 45-pound bar, totaled 135 pounds. Not bad for a little 35-plus guy like me. Though it was difficult, I was able to do 10 repetitions with some strength to spare.

Feeling inspired, I put on additional 10-pound plates, for a total of 155 pounds. Again, it was difficult, especially the last three repetitions, but I pressed another 10 reps. Surely I could do a little more. I found some 5-pound plates and was now up to 165 pounds.

Grabbing the bar for my third set, I pushed with all my might to lift it off the rests. Breathe in, push up, down easy, air out...one. Breathe in, push up, down easy, air out...two. Breathe in, push up, down easy, air out...three. And so on to 10. The last four or five reps were extremely tough. (In lifting terms, toughness is directly proportional to the facial contortions and guttural sounds one makes.) But I did it!

As I started to walk away, the chest-pounding maleness in me kicked in one more time. I figured I could do more. Surely, I could do 175. It was just 10 pounds more. I found two more 5-pound plates, and as I added them to the bar, I thought about getting a spotter—someone to be there just in case I was unable to lift the weight off my chest. Nah, I had just done 10 reps at 165 pounds, and 175 pounds was just a fraction more. How hard could that be?

Lying on the bench once again, I placed my hands on the bar, closed my eyes, and envisioned lifting a feather. I told myself it was only 10 more pounds. I filled my lungs to capacity and, using my diaphragm for support, gave a tremendous push to get the bar off its launchpad. With 175 pounds above my chest, held up by two locked arms, I thought about the task at hand. Either I would successfully lift the bar or I would crush my chest. I couldn't turn back. I had to forge ahead.

I let the bar down slowly until it nearly touched my chest and then gave a tremendous push. The bar went up a few inches and stalled. "Uh oh!" I thought. "You're a volcano!" I told myself. "Erupt!" I strained to get the bar higher, but couldn't. I felt my arms weaken further. As they were about to buckle, a guy nearby came over and asked if I needed help. "Yes, yes," I stammered, as the thought of concave pectorals flashed through my mind.

After getting the bar back on the rests, I thanked the man for his help. As he turned to walk away, he suggested that I get a spotter next time.

How Much Are Your Employees Lifting?

This tale is about sensitivity to the backgrounds and experiences of others, about understanding that another's life journey affects how that person interprets the "weight" of events.

Every now and then an incident in the workplace appears "light" and innocuous to some but is significantly "heavy" and disturbing to others. You know what I'm talking about. It's the innocent "I didn't mean anything by it" gay joke told in the lunchroom. It's having a brand-new refrigerator in the air-conditioned main office area where mostly college grads work and an older refrigerator near the hot assembly line where many high school grads work. It's having calendars of scantily clad women on walls and locker room doors. In the big scheme of things, and taken as singular, disconnected events, these things might be seen as trivial.

If you are the one who makes the joke, who has the good fridge, or who puts up the calendar, you probably would perceive your actions as innocent. If an offended party were to complain, you would tell him or her to lighten up, to quit being so sensitive. It is unlikely that you would think about why that person finds it so offensive. It is equally unlikely that you would think of these "isolated" incidents as links in a long chain of connected events. You would see "light" where others see "heavy."

But my trip to the gym shows how the weight of an event can be differently felt. So-called out-group people, such as minorities, homosexuals, the homeless, and those in poverty, carry an accumulated weight of discrimination and exclusion. Years of being left on the fringes are like the 30-minute bike ride. They tire you out. Often, you exert lots of energy trying to make your way up the societal or workplace ladder, but you make little progress because of built-in, systemic barriers.

Already tired, you then have to endure the reality that you don't have access to the same doors others walk through easily. Maybe the barrier is your age, the color of your skin, or your socioeconomic status. Maybe it's your gender or sexual orientation. Whatever your marker is, society has turned the things that identify you into that original 155 pounds of weight that limits what you can pursue and achieve. You press on while trying to make the in-group recognize the reality of the additional weights you are holding up. Very few in-group members hear and see how tough it is. They let you know, through various overt and subtle means, that they think your pain is imaginary or blown out of proportion. The process of persuading others that the barrier in your path is real serves as the 10-pound plates that continue to zap your energy. Your muscles are now burning, but you don't give up.

Next, weight is added when others who you thought "got it" don't follow through on the commitment they so passionately made to do something. You find out that their passion exists only in attitude, not in behavior. They tell you to not make a big fuss because they don't want to ruffle the organizational feathers, to create a hostile environment for the majority. It's really hard now with an additional five pounds on either side, but you don't give up.

Finally, under the stress of being invisible, unheard, and marginalized, the last five-pound weights—the "playful" jokes about women's work, the "nice" comments about being "so articulate," or the "innocent" references to "those lazy people"—load on. You have no more energy to lift the bar, let alone hold it up. The bar comes crashing down and everybody sees. But people don't see the cumulative weight and burden. They see only the last little weights that you tried to lift. And because they are unable or unwilling to see the whole truth, they can't and won't serve as the much-needed spotter that all of us need when things get rough.

The weight of an environment that is not as inclusive as it could be is extremely heavy. It takes only a little incident to make the proverbial mountain out of a molehill. And when that happens, the whole organization suffers. Some companies are hit with lawsuits. Just ask Coca-Cola, Texaco, and Denny's. Others suffer because they have to take time away from core activities to deal with issues that could have been resolved using proactive measures—or by more people taking on the responsibility of being attentive spotters.

Do you have what it takes to be a spotter? Are you sensitive enough to others' viewpoints and experiences to understand how a molehill becomes a mountain? And are you strong enough to argue for the mountain when the majority of people around you see only a molehill? If your answer is no, you may want to make some new personal goals on this front. If you achieve your goals, I think you'll be pleasantly surprised at the image you see the next time you look in the mirror.

And you won't even have to smell a locker room in the process.

Being a Better "Spotter"

Opening our eyes so we can see the weights and be the spotter takes time and energy. To help start you on the journey of better "spotting," here are some questions to ask, an activity, and an assignment for this week.

1. **First glance.** What invisible weights have you seen come crashing down on someone in your organization? What "molehills" have left you puzzled, uncertain as to why it was such a "big deal"? What information or perspective might you be missing?

2. **Looking inward.** Think about your behavior when someone is burdened. Are you a "spotter," or do you add weight? Or do you perhaps do both, in different circumstances? Do you watch from the sideline, or step in to help?

3. **What if?** What if some people get more spotters than others? What if some people get no spotter?

4. **Activity.** In a group exercise or confidentially in a survey, ask people what are some invisible or visible "weights" in your organization. Who gets the most spotters in your workplace? Then, as a group, explore how those weights are both burdens and opportunities, and brainstorm ideas for how one might be an effective spotter in each situation.

5. **This week's assignment.** Critically examine your environments and the people in them, searching for invisible weights you have often overlooked. Then identify one person for whom you can start "spotting"—and begin.

| 10 |

Clothes Hoarder

I think I might have an issue with clothes. I'll bet some of you suffer from this same issue. Many of us have lots of clothes we never wear. Personally, it's not even a case of clothes we *rarely* wear. I actually *never* wear them, but there they sit in the drawers of my dresser and hang on the racks in my closet. I just can't seem to get rid of them. It's been suggested I could open up my own used-clothing store with the inventory I have in stock. The person I committed to spend the rest of my life with has told me that I must get rid of an item of clothing for every item that I purchase. Okay, I could have a problem.

I become aware of this little problem every so often when I hear stories about people who hoard things. It seems that there are people in this world who can't break the relationship they have with items they've accumulated. Apparently, there is a lot of these people, or at least a lot of interest in these folks, because there's a television program aptly called *Hoarders.* It's a peculiar show that allows viewers to see what happens when one has attachment issues with things that no longer have any functional value. The program doesn't seem like it would be interesting, but somehow it sucks you in, much like the Kardashians. It's literally not a pretty sight (I leave it up to you to decide whether I'm talking about *Hoarders* or the sisters), at least to those of us who call ourselves normal. And since I see myself as fairly normal and never want to play the starring role on *Hoarders*, I occasionally find myself motivated to purge excess items from my wardrobe.

On these occasions, I dive into lessening my sartorial load with great conviction, committing myself to eliminating clothing items that can be carbon-dated to the 1980s. The process is similar every time. The last episode went something like this: I begin with my closet. Pregnant with sport coats and suits, I pluck off coat jackets that I haven't worn for years. A few are too big, but I think they'll fit nicely if I get back to regularly working out as I was doing in my twenties. Some are too small, easily remedied by reducing a few calories from my daily intake. One jacket has a tear in it. *This one should definitely be tossed*, I think to myself. But as I am about to make it the first item in the "get rid of" pile, I fondly recall my eighth-grade Home Economics class where I learned to sew. I set it aside for future repair. I then eye a suit I had purchased on a business trip I took to Italy nearly 10 years ago. The jacket is Caribbean blue, body hugging but with enough stretch to keep me comfortable if I ever decided I needed to strike a bodybuilding pose. The matching pants that accompanied the jacket were prototypical Italian, stylishly narrow and ankle length. It hasn't adorned my body in the United States. It should probably be tossed. But that suit would come in handy if I make it to Italy again. And I remind myself, this is a real Italian suit made and bought in a little tailor's shop in Italy, not some suit I picked up in a US store that was made in some Italian factory. Moreover, it was expensive. The one-of-a kind blue Italian suit gets to stay a while longer in my closet. And so it goes. Many items could be evicted from my closet, but my "get rid of" pile has no more than a couple of items. I should be disappointed that my closet is about as full as when I started, but I am not. This exercise has flooded my brain with dopamine, and that is good enough.

My reluctance and inability to detach myself from clothes I no longer wear is an example of what psychologists refer to as the *Sunk Cost Fallacy.* Simply put, it is a cognitive distortion that makes it difficult for us to let go of things in which we have invested resources, even when those things no longer have functional or utilitarian value. The brain places value on things that we have invested time, energy, and money into and has a problem with getting rid of things it values, even when those things do not have actual value, or even negative value. The brain is loss-averse. The Sunk Cost Fallacy helps to explain why some people find it nearly impossible to get out of bad relationships. For these people, they see a relationship in which they've highly invested, and in their minds, it would be a waste to give up on the relationship. So, they'll create internal stories that offer a better, more valuable future state as a means for rationalizing why they have not walked away. The Sunk Cost Fallacy is often a big psychological factor that can help us understand why many entrepreneurs sink more and more money into a failing business even when all objective data says, "Let It Go!" They, as the saying goes, "throw good money after bad."

For organizations, the Sunk Cost Fallacy sheds light on why some patterns and processes that have been in place for a long time are hard to get rid of, even when there is a better way to do things. For example, consider an organization that has invested a lot of resources into a software platform that, while exceptional at first, has become clunky and inefficient. Better, more current software platforms exist, but people in the organization would have to learn any new platform purchased. Many in the organization resist because they "sunk" a lot of time to learn the older software. So instead of adopting and adapting to any new software platform that would actually be more efficient and save money, the organization sticks with the legacy platform, putting together customized add-on components that actually cost the organization even more money. Even with objective information that indicates that they'd be better off with purchasing new software, they make the irrational decision to stick with the old software because they've "sunk" significant resources into it over the years.

The Sunk Cost Fallacy can also help to explain why it's hard to get rid of poorly performing, or even toxic, employees. The organization has sunk so many resources into salary, training, and maybe into the relationship, that it can cloud their judgment when it comes to letting that person go. So, they'll sink more money and resources into the employee, even when it is objectively clear that a change must be made. Consider a situation in which it comes to light that an employee has sexually harassed another employee. It is relatively easy for the powers that be to play down or overlook a complaint, especially when the harasser has been with the organization for a number of years. According to the Sunk Cost Fallacy, the calculus goes like this: We invested (sunk) a lot of time, money, and energy into this employee. Getting rid of him or her would be a waste of all that investment. Let's give this person another chance. So, the organization holds on to this person, rationalizing away the negative and sinking more resources into this person.

The Sunk Cost Fallacy, combined with the brain's aversion for loss, leads to many irrational decisions we make when deciding whether to let go of things we've invested a lot of resources in. Whether it's people, objects, or even beliefs and ideas, we can easily talk ourselves into holding on to things that no longer have value. I do this with clothes. I'm not as bad as those really bad, irrational people they depict on the television show *Hoarders*. I have very good, rational reasons for keeping T-shirts and sweatshirts from my college years. Though I haven't worn them for decades, maybe one of my four kids will wear them when they attend my alma mater. I'm holding on to those T-shirts for them. It's all about them.

Examining Sunken Cost Fallacy

To help you be more mindful of when you may need to let some things go when they no longer have value, here are some questions to ask, an activity, and an assignment for this week.

1. **First glance.** What's your quick reaction to "Sunken Cost Fallacy," the idea that we tend to hang on to things that have little or no value to us?

2. **Looking inward.** How does Sunken Cost Fallacy lead you to hold on to things you should let go of, whether these things be objects, resources, or potentially harmful relationships? What's the cost of holding on?

3. **What if?** What if you and your organization could overcome Sunken Cost Fallacy, what would you jettison? Why?

4. **Activity.** In a small group, discuss how Sunken Cost Fallacy can harm a team or an organization.

5. **This week's assignment.** Go through your physical and mental closet and try to get rid of things that no longer have value. Note the emotions and thoughts you might have during and after this process.

REVISING
MENTAL
MODELS

"While walls can serve to protect,
they can also isolate and imprison."
—Steve L. Robbins

| 11 |

A Bunch of Noise

Are you a good friend? According to a high school buddy of mine, the answer to that question lies in your willingness to tell a person that they have food in their teeth. And he wasn't referring to a tiny piece of black pepper. No, he meant the big, distracting blob of spinach or kale that commands attention in the midst of a face-to-face conversation. Set aside that embarrassing mental image for a second, and you'd have to admit that my friend's litmus test for friendship strength has *some* validity.

The problem, as you're realizing, is that you can't let go of that image. If you're like most people, you are now thinking about that green blob! It just hijacked your mind. You're thinking of all the times you've been in that situation. You're trying to recall what you did on those occasions. Or you're checking your teeth right now, just to make sure *you* aren't the one presently in need of a good friend. This mental image is what we in the field of communication call "noise."

Noise, technically, is anything that might prevent you from getting your message across to another the way you originally desired. It's a message, verbal or nonverbal, that's not interpreted by the receiver the way the sender intended. Most people think of noise in terms of physical loudness, as measured in decibels. Ever wonder how loud some things are? A normal conversation takes place at about 60 decibels. An average gas-engine lawnmower is fairly loud, at something near 100 decibels. Within 10 feet, a jet engine attacks your eardrums at 140 decibels—definitely deafening!

Sometimes, however, noise has nothing to do with decibels. Noise can be something psychological or emotional caused by something physical. It can be that disgusting green blob of spinach in someone's teeth that you can't stop looking at. It's akin to a Justin Bieber song. You know you shouldn't listen, but you end up doing it anyway. Or, it's your boss's receding hairline that he tries to cover up with the "comb-over." While these things have nothing to do with physical loudness, they are also noise.

Noise can be understood as distractions that cause misunderstandings, disruptions that block goal attainment, and perceptual filters that create misjudgment. In a workplace setting, noise then can be the tattoo or body piercing that causes you to underestimate the ability of a young coworker, or even an older one. It can be the style of someone's clothing that doesn't fit your perceptions of appropriate dress (emphasis on "your"). Noise can be another's accent that conjures up thoughts of snobby, arrogant people. Noise can range from a person's skin color to their gender to even which department they work in. It can be the type of educational degree one has or doesn't have.

Noise can be as simple as another person's name. For example, my wife (once a schoolteacher) and I had a very difficult time naming our children. Whenever I would mention a name, say *Jeffrey*, my wife would mention, "No, I once had a Jeffrey as a student, and he was difficult to deal with. Our kid can't be named Jeffrey." Then I would offer up *James*. "We can't have a James," my wife would say. "I had a James one year. I wouldn't wish him upon anyone." And it would go on and on. It's a miracle our four kids have first names.

To understand how noise influences us, it might be helpful to think of noise and its impact similar to how a sound engineer views noise. Sound engineers are concerned about signal-to-noise ratio (S/N). In most cases, they want to decrease the amount of noise that might exist in a signal because noise operates to attenuate the clarity of the signal. In other words, noise hides parts of the signal. When it comes to people, noise can have a similar effect. Noise can hide talent. One person may not be able to get past another's accent to see how smart they are. Another person can't reconcile someone's sexual orientation to realize how hard-working and talented they are. Still another isn't able to overcome a person's type or lack of a particular educational degree to appreciate their innovative ideas.

Interestingly, noise not only has the ability to hide talent; it can also hide a lack of talent. A lot of research suggests that perceived physical attractiveness influences our judgment of the competency in others. In other words, we might overrate a person's writing ability because we think of them as attractive, and vice versa. Unless you can make the case that physical attractiveness is causally, or even in a correlational sense, related to writing ability, then what you have is noise. The type of educational degree one has can also hide a lack of talent. Just because a person holds a degree from an Ivy League school does not mean that individual is competent for the job you are asking them to do.

So how can you and I overcome the limiting effects of the noise that exists all around us? First, it's helpful to remind ourselves that noise resides in the person making the judgment of the target. Noise does not reside within the target. In other words, think of noise as something that's in us (not them) but prevents us from seeing or understanding others the way they want to be seen and understood. Second, we must become more aware and take inventory of the types of noise (i.e., biased mental models, opinions, beliefs) we have within us that can distort our thinking and interpretations of others and others' ideas. Finally, we can practice becoming more mindful of intentionally addressing noise by challenging ourselves to learn more about others we presently deem to be "noisy."

So, the question we began with, "How good a friend are you?" is actually a coded question for how well you are able to overcome and break through all of the noise you might experience in encounters with others. Are you willing to work to become more aware of the subtle noises that often lie beneath our level of awareness? If not, make it a point to become more aware. Make a list. Take some time with coworkers to identify the types of noise that inhabit your particular workplace. I think you'll find there are many, and that many of the issues you face at work are the result of the noise you identify.

By the way, my high school buddy, you know, the one with the litmus test for relationships? He pondered other significant things, such as, "A good poop is often underrated." Now, there's some more mental noise for the rest of your day.

Minimizing the Negative Effects of Noise

To help you recognize and minimize the noise that can prevent you from seeing and understanding others the way they'd like to be seen and understood, here are some questions to ask, an activity, and an assignment for this week.

1. **First glance.** What operates like noise in your organization? Consider aspects of people (i.e., dimensions of diversity) that can have the effect of hiding talent as well as lack of talent. How has/does noise impact your organization in the competition for twenty-first-century talent?

2. **Looking inward.** What types of noise operate within you? How does noise influence the way you interact with people in the workplace? Home? Community?

3. **What if?** What if your organization took a critical look at "noise" and its effects on the workplace? What are some potential outcomes of such an examination, both negative and positive?

4. **Activity.** In a small group, ask people to list five things that they believe are noise. Compare people's lists to see if there are commonalities. Have a conversation about your lists and any commonalities they may have.

5. **This week's assignment.** On a piece of paper, write down one thing that operates as noise to you that you would like to address this week. Find ways to keep whatever you wrote down at the top of your mind and practice discovering what might be hidden behind the noise as you encounter people that your brain considers to be "noisy."

| 12 |

"Bizeer Gummies"

"So, guys, what would you like for a snack before bedtime?" I asked as my three sons and I drove home one night. Nicholas and Zachary, the two eldest, quickly responded in unison: "Fruit roll-ups!"

"Now, there's good eating," I thought. I looked back at Jacob, our 2-year-old, who hadn't yet put in his order. He seemed to be processing an algorithm in deciding what he wanted. "What would you like, Jacob?"

"Umm, umm, umm...bizeer gummies."

"What kind of gummies?" I asked for clarification.

"Bizeer gummies!" he said confidently.

I searched my brain's toddler-to-adult language translation database. Nothing. What in the heck are "bizeer gummies"? Maybe I was losing my hearing. Should have listened when my mom warned me about going to Bee Gees and Andy Gibb concerts.

"Can you say that again, Jacob? What would you like for a snack?"

"Bizeer gummies!" he said again, this time with a look and tone that made me feel like I was the language-challenged person in this dialogue. "I want bizeer gummies."

I have a PhD in communication, yet I was floundering. What could this young alien be talking about? I had encountered other alien forms of communication in the past with my first two sons, but this was a different dialect. "Gummies" I understood. But "bizeer" did not register.

"Say it one more time, Jacob. What would you like for a snack?"

I turned my head to see Jacob scowling at me with eyebrows furrowed. "I WANT BIZEER GUMMIES!"

Still nothing. Just as I was about to throw in the translation towel, a voice piped up from the back of our minivan, "I know what Jacob wants." Speaking with a calmness that belied my true feelings, I asked Nicholas, my eldest son, why he hadn't said something sooner. All I got back was, "I don't know." He's not even a teenager and already he doesn't know things.

"So, what does Jacob want, Nicholas?"

"He wants Buzz Lightyear gummies," my son responded nonchalantly, as if to suggest that I had received my PhD by mail order.

"Of course, Buzz Lightyear gummies," I said to myself. It made perfect sense. My epiphany came just as we pulled into our driveway.

When I got in the house, I asked my wife if she knew what "bizeer gummies" were, just to reassure myself that other adults also are ignorant about toddler talk. "Of course!" she said with that how-did-men-come-to-run-the-world? look. "Bizeer gummies are Buzz Lightyear gummies. You would know that if you did more grocery shopping with your sons."

Ouch! Ouch! and Ouch! In a span of 10 minutes my youngest son had taught me how frustrating it can be when one is not well understood, and my dear, loving wife had underscored the fact that to understand others, you must get to know them. And to get to know them, you must take intentional steps to spend time with them.

Who Are Your "Aliens"?

We've all heard it said that you can't understand what you don't know. But how many of us take to heart the fundamental lesson in that statement? To get to know people, you have to interact with them. And by interact, I do not mean exchanging polite, yet insincere, "drive-by" hellos while passing in the hall at work. Real, substantive interaction means taking time to hang out, to communicate, and to learn about one another.

Fundamentally, communication is the process of creating shared meaning and understanding. Even in this age of proliferating electronic communication, there is no substitute for face-to-face contact when developing relationships. The more time we spend with others, the more we tend to learn about them. The more we learn about them, the greater the chance that there will be fewer misunderstandings between us. Strangers become less strange. So, investing time in communicating with others is like taking out an insurance policy against lack of understanding in the future.

It's hard to set aside time for people we don't know. But with the United States becoming more racially and culturally diverse, it is imperative that individuals and organizations that want to be culturally competent take out that insurance policy. The more time we invest, the greater the chance we will learn that we have a lot in common, or that substantive differences are launchpads for greater learning.

When we don't take the time to create shared meaning and

understanding, we assure ourselves of future communication problems. Misunderstanding and lack of understanding often result in frustration and anger for all parties. It doesn't take a rocket scientist, or even a PhD in communication, to recognize that frustrated and angry people generally are not beneficial to organizations.

It's in the best interest of organizations to encourage an investment in building relationships among their personnel, on and off the clock. And that means relationship building not just between people who feel comfortable with each other, but also between people who don't find a lot in common right away. It's with these "other" people that the potential for lack of understanding and misunderstanding is highest.

This failure in understanding often occurs when there is "noise" in the message transfer. By noise, I mean anything that hinders the receiver from getting the message the sender intended. Noise can be anything from a language barrier to distracting nonverbal signs to having lenses and filters that distort the message. Noise is not necessarily anyone's fault. But we must recognize it as a cause of communication problems, and we must overcome it if we are to achieve effective communication.

A combination of factors contributed to the noise between Jacob and me. One factor was my lack of the correct filter to decipher the word "bizeer." Another was my son's way of pronouncing words, which did not fit my method and style of oral communication. Neither Jacob nor I can do much to muffle these types of noise. So I am left with only one course of action if I want to fix the noise problem immediately: I need to spend more time with Jacob, to get to know him and his method of communication better.

It's really just that simple to overcome "understanding" problems with others who may communicate or act a little differently from the way we do. Yep, that's right, we need to allocate more time to getting to know others. By building relationships, we will foster an environment in which creating shared meaning is more possible and reaching mutual understanding is more likely.

So take out that insurance policy and get to know others with whom you rarely spend time. But remember, insurance policies mature over time with regular payments. In the same way, relationships are built over time, with regular and frequent payments of attention. It's hard work that often yields lasting benefits.

Getting Rid of the Noise

Is it time to cut down on the noise? To achieve noise reduction for yourself and your organization, here are some questions to ask, an activity, and an assignment for this week.

1. **First glance.** Identify situations or procedures in your organization that are unclear, that you have difficulty understanding. What clouds the message? What pieces are you missing that might impair your ability to understand?

2. **Looking inward.** Have you ever found yourself misunderstood? How did you feel at that moment? What were the unintentional outcomes of that situation?

3. **What if?** What if you can't understand the accent of or relate to a new coworker or neighbor because of some noise (e.g., different age, nationality, style of dress, etc.)? Are you trying your best to understand and relate? To be understood?

4. **Activity.** Recording your group's responses on a flip chart, identify some of the noise in your organizational communication style. Identify some of the unspoken rules/norms that exist in your organization's culture. How are managers and supervisors ensuring that everyone hears the same message? Give specific examples of how an employee orientation program might incorporate tools for understanding for all new employees. What can your organization do to eliminate some of its noise?

5. **This week's assignment.** Start to make payments of time and effort on your relational insurance policy with one person who thinks, communicates, or acts a little differently from the way you do.

| 13 |

Inaccurate Maps

"Where could this place be?" I said to myself as I drove around in my little rental car at 9:30 p.m., searching for my hotel. According to the map and directions I had been given, my destination was somewhere on Grand Street. But Grand Street was nowhere to be found. If I had been looking for Jackson, Washington, or Jefferson Street, or some other street named after a US president, I would have been just fine. But I was not fine. The instructions in my hand said nothing about those streets. All they provided were the basics: "Get off the highway, turn right on Central Avenue, drive a few miles, then turn right on Grand Street. The hotel is on the right." As I drove farther and farther I became more and more frustrated. I was consoled, however, by the thought that if I ever wanted a street named after me, all I had to do was become president of the United States.

With my anxiety level rising, I thought about stopping to ask for directions. Of course, that thought quickly drowned in a torrent of testosterone. After all, I am male, and there are certain male stereotypes that I am called to live up to mindlessly. Stopping for directional assistance would be tantamount to raising the white flag of defeat. (I'm quite sure the person stuck driving behind me at 20 mph in a 40-mph zone would have gladly raised the flag for me and waved it with great vigor.)

After driving another 10 minutes or so with no Grand Street in sight, I pulled over to the side of the road to get my bearings. Understand that I was not stopping to ask for help. I was just stopping to get a better look at my map and directions. (There is a big difference between stopping and stopping to ask for directions, a distinction made clear in the Males' Secret Rules Book.)

Sitting in my decidedly spartan rental car as other vehicles whizzed by, I was so anxious and nervous that I was shaking. I needed more information, more details to soothe my uncertainty. Studying the map to get a better orientation to and understanding of this unfamiliar environment, I looked to see if I had missed anything—a landmark, a street, or some other identifying detail. But I couldn't find any additional information that could assist me.

Now what was I going to do? It was late and dark, and I didn't know where I was. At such times I have learned to stop, take a breather, and offer up a succinct but powerful prayer. Though the words are slightly different each time, the message is basically the same: "I don't know where I am going, God. I need your help."

So, with my prayer offered up, I turned back onto Central Avenue, driving with a little less anxiety but still lost. Within 30 seconds, my prayer was answered. To my left was a big billboard advertising a restaurant at my hotel. At the bottom of the billboard was the information I needed: "Right on Grand Street, 3 Miles Ahead."

"Yippee," I blurted, just as my 3-year-old son does when his prayer for a chocolate-covered donut with sprinkles is answered in the affirmative. I would be in a nice hotel room soon.

How Good Are Your Maps?

It has been said that we live in a world of territories and maps. Territories are the actual physical places that exist in our three-dimensional world. Maps are the two-dimensional representations of those territories. Maps vary in accuracy. Obviously, the more accurate a map is, the easier it is for the map's user to find a particular location.

Just as we can have bad maps of real territories, we often have bad "people maps" that give us inaccurate or incomplete information about others. If our people maps are bad enough, when we actually encounter the real thing we have a tendency to become anxious, uncertain, disoriented, or even fearful. And in those emotional states, we are more likely to react negatively than positively. We are more likely to be exclusive than inclusive. We are more likely to submit to our stereotypical maps than to embrace the reality of the "people territory." In other words, if we are programmed with incomplete maps (as we all generally are when it comes to people who are different from us) and we make no attempt to create more accurate maps, then we should not be surprised to find ourselves frustrated and fearful during encounters with others.

As our world becomes increasingly diverse, we all would do well to create and develop more accurate people maps. Doing so means we must expose ourselves to as many different people territories as possible. There is no shortcut. No book you can read, no play you can attend, no PBS program you can watch will take the place of direct interaction with different kinds of people. These are easy substitutes that we often use to rationalize our less-than-pioneering spirit. Any substitute, by definition, is just another map that lacks the critical details.

In the process of acquiring better maps, we likely will find ourselves in a better position to embrace the diversity around us. With better maps, we will be more likely to see that differences in others are not necessarily better or worse—just different. We likely will discover a vein of gold instead of chunks of coal. Maybe then we will look around and discover that we don't even need maps anymore because we know the territories so well.

Developing Better People Maps

Let's critically examine our people maps (i.e., mental models of people) and see if we can discover new ways of navigating unfamiliar territories. To help you get started, here are some questions to ask, an activity, and an assignment for this week.

1. **First glance.** Examine the organization chart for your organization and identify the people maps pertaining to different groups or departments. How accurate are they? Now take a broader look. How accurate are the people maps that are represented in the media?

2. **Looking inward.** What people maps were you brought up to believe were representative of real territories? Based on those maps, what thoughts, assumptions, and attributes do you assign to people at first glance? How might getting to know someone make a difference?

3. **What if?** What if, in our encounters with new people and new perspectives, we paused and calmly asked, "What help might I need to better understand?" What if we actually visited real territories instead of always relying on maps? What if occasional discomfort is needed in order to learn about the "other"?

˙Developing Better People Maps (cont'd)

4. **Activity.** Divide the group into several smaller groups. Ask each small group to take a piece of paper and list on it some of its members' people maps. As the groups jot down their maps, ask them to identify where their maps came from and note the impact they have had on their members' ability to navigate new territories. Discuss various maps within the groups, sharing their influence and impact. Did some people have the same map or very similar maps? Did others have very different maps? Did anyone in the groups have all the possible maps? How can differences in maps be a source of frustration—or creativity? What can we learn about our accumulated information?

5. **This week's assignment.** Pick one person or group of people. Toss out your old map about that individual or group and replace it with a sincere effort to navigate and understand a three-dimensional territory.

| 14 |
Harmless Images?

A friend once told me a story that I find enlightening, especially as a parent. This friend, an American Indian, has a son who, at 8 years old, enjoyed watching cowboys-and-Indians movies on television.

Before the start of a show, the boy would dress up in traditional American Indian clothing, proudly putting on the authentic garments his grandmother had made for him. Of course, he also would get something to snack on before he plopped down in front of the screen; he didn't miss a moment of these shows.

The father, pleased that his son was wearing traditional Native dress, didn't pay attention to the content of the programs at first. He soon would take notice.

One day, the father came home to find his son watching another cowboys-and-Indians program. As usual, his son sat about three feet from the television, munching chips. But this time something was different. Instead of Native clothing, the boy was wearing a cowboy hat and

91

had a bandana tied around his neck. A plastic rifle was at his side, where he generally kept a play bow and arrow.

"Son," my friend said, "usually when you watch these shows you dress in our Native clothing. I am so proud when you do that. Why are you dressed like a cowboy today?"

The boy looked at his dad and said matter-of-factly, "Sometimes I wanna win, too, Dad."

When I heard this story, I was filled with sadness. I couldn't help but think how those cowboys-and-Indians movies had affected the boy's psyche and self-esteem, and how they continue to mold the minds of all children (and adults) who watch them.

Viewing these types of programs over and over again, as my friend's son had, we gradually develop images in our mind about who are "winners" and who are "losers," about who is superior and who is inferior.

What's on Your Mental Screen?

Sadly, shows like this continue to intrigue people today, just as they did several generations that preceded them. And most of these viewers have never had any significant, meaningful interaction with an American Indian! So, many of the images of American Indians in our society— how we see them and think of them—have come from indirect sources, often based on incomplete, inaccurate, and biased information.

Whether we learned it from movies, television shows, teachers, faith institutions, storybooks, or even parents, the way we view American Indians is more likely a stereotype than reality, more myth than truth.

As I said, there are now several generations of adults who grew up watching shows that portray American Indians and other people of color in stereotypically negative roles with off-putting characteristics. And despite efforts to refute such negative portrayals, many of these adults undoubtedly carry images of American Indians that reflect the stock characters they saw on television or read about in books.

We all must challenge ourselves to get the "truth, the whole truth, and nothing but the truth" about American Indians. Only then might we begin to understand why many people take offense at schools' use of "Indian" mascots and other manifestations of cultural stereotyping.

Revising the Screenplay

If we are to change what we see on our mental screen, we first must know what is currently showing there. To help you understand and revise your inner screenplay, here are some questions to ask, an activity, and an assignment for this week.

1. **First glance.** Who are the heroes in your organization? What do they look like? Does your organization seem to favor a certain model of leaders? Of line workers? Of office staff?

2. **Looking inward.** Who are the winners and losers in your mental model? How do these pictures influence the attributes you assign to various groups of people?

3. **What if?** What if one group wins more often than the rest? What if our societal structure allows some to be more suited for winning than others? What if we really don't live in a meritocracy and some people achieve success because of factors other than hard work? What if everyone does not have equal access to the same relationships, connections, and opportunities?

4. **Activity.** In a group, make a list of eight to 10 leadership attributes. At first glance, do these attributes tend to favor one group more than another? Now make a list of the behavioral traits we teach boys and a list of those we teach girls. How do the lists compare to your list of leadership attributes? Is one group more conditioned than the other to excel in a leadership role as you've defined it? What does this tell you about your mental model of a leader? Can anyone be a winner in your organization, or does a person have to "dress up" a particular way to win?

5. **This week's assignment.** Critically examine various media (e.g., television, magazines, radio, internet, newspapers) from the perspective of an underrepresented group. Write down some insights from your observations, and then perhaps share them with others.

| 15 |

Messages, Meat-eaters, and Mental Models—Oh My!

Look at my picture. No, really, look. Okay. Now you may read on. But before you do, let me get a few stereotypes out of the way that may be running through your head about me. First, I don't know karate, kung fu, tae kwon do, or any other martial art. I've never owned or worked at a Laundromat, nor any restaurant for that matter. Ladies, I can't give you a manicure, and guys, you definitely don't want me tailoring your clothes. And while I enjoy math and science, I am not an engineer, and Newton's Three Laws of Motion are about as deep as I go in a discussion of physics.

If you are like many people, you've had some type of cognitive or emotional reaction to the Asian stereotypes that I mentioned. Some of you laughed or giggled. Others of you may have bristled, thinking that a "diversity professional" like myself should know better than to mention race-based stereotypes in such a manner. I'm pretty darn sure none of you were clueless about what I was talking about. You've heard the stereotypes before. When you have a reaction to these stereotypes, whether positive or negative, what that tells me—and what that should tell you—about *you* is that you have stereotypes in your head about people we call Asians. I have the same ones in my head. And here's the deal: these stereotypes (what I'll also refer to as mental models) that exist in our heads do not necessarily arise from formal study or any type of intense conscious learning effort on our part. The recognition that there are Asian stereotypes (or any other stereotypes) dotting our cognitive landscape might lead you to ask, "How did those ideas get there?" and, "How do they influence me?"

Let's take the first question, "How did they get there?" While we can formally study Asians with the goal of embedding stereotypes in our head, it's my guess that none of us did. None of us had to purchase the *Dummies' Guide to Asian Stereotypes* (hmm, I hope no such a book exists) and study it for hours on end like we were cramming for an exam. No, all we have to do is live in an environment that gives us limited, narrow messages about people we regularly refer to as Asians. Repeated exposures to such messages, without exposure to different messages, slowly builds mental models for us. We absorb these stereotype-building messages in the same way that we absorb the lyrics of a song. You have songs and their associated verses and choruses not because you studied them, but because you heard them repeatedly. Moreover, you didn't even have to pay attention to the songs as they wafted through the air and into your ears. Your brain grabs the words for you, outside of your awareness.

The "absorption" of messages is actually a natural cognitive process.

Our brain is constantly gathering information from the environment, building a database of cognitive models and mental representations of the world. It uses these mental models as a way of quickly and efficiently understanding its surroundings. The mental models also serve as reference points for making sense of people, objects, and things that you encounter. This cognitive process was essential for survival for our ancestors. Rapid assessments of environments were not optional long ago. They were crucial for survival. Think about how long our ancestors would have lasted if they had not created good mental models of MEAT-EATERS! You could say we are the descendants of those who built accurate mental models and used them well!

As you might imagine, we have lots of mental models in our heads, of Asians, Democrats and Republicans, First Nation people, gays, Christians, Muslims, Americans, poor and rich people, engineers, people with tattoos, and so on. Now the question is: How do these mental models influence us? In its continuous effort to conserve energy, our brain uses mental models to make quick judgments and decisions about people and things with which it engages. Think of mental models as an integral piece of the stimulus-response process. Our brain draws information from the mental model to inform a response. For our ancestors, MEAT-EATER (stimulus) meant RUN (response).

Most of us don't live in the same hostile environment that our ancestors found themselves in, but our brain works in pretty much the same way—building mental models in order to inform judgments and decision making. Think ASIAN MALE (stimulus) knows KARATE (mental response). But just as our ancestors made mistakes in judgment, so do we. WOMAN does not necessarily mean NOT STRONG LEADER. POOR does not necessarily mean LAZY. MUSLIM does not necessarily mean TERRORIST. EDUCATED does not necessarily mean WISE. TATTOOS do not necessarily mean LAW-BREAKER. Just because we have the ability to build mental models does not guarantee that we always build accurate ones. Mental models built on narrow, limited information often form our stereotypes and associated biases, from which we mindlessly judge and evaluate others. Consequently, mistakes in judgment and evaluation can easily occur.

I am sure you have heard people say things like, "I don't have a prejudiced bone in my body" or "I don't have any biases." Well, now you know that these people know not of what they speak. You can tell them they really don't know how the human brain works. The question is not whether or not we have prejudice or biases. Cognitive science clearly says we do—for a very good reason. The real question—for we who see ourselves as open-minded, caring, compassionate people—is how do our cognitive-based biases impact and influence our understanding and judgments of other people and their ideas. How do my biases influence me to see my friends and "insiders" differently than I see strangers and "outsiders"? Could my mental models impact me to give the benefit of the doubt to some (insiders) and be skeptical of others (outsiders) even when all else is equal? And could all this be happening without me consciously knowing?

It takes mindful effort and a lot of cognitive energy to examine how our biases and prejudices (built on narrow, limited messages) play themselves out minute-by-minute, day-by-day. But, if we are intent on judging people more accurately and treating people more fairly, we must become more mindful. To minimize unintentional intolerance and mindless exclusion, we will need to engage in the effortful process of critically examining ourselves and then getting to know others beyond superficial cues and inaccurate mental models. If we are serious about inclusion then we must also be serious about understanding ourselves and our mental models better.

Ultimately, it's about building relationships and caring about others who may exist outside our mental and physical comfort zones. It just may turn out that those scary MEAT-EATERS are less dangerous than we've been led to believe. The outsiders, less strange and less different once we get to know them. Heck, what if it's the case that the more we get beyond limiting stereotypes and less than optimal mental models and begin caring more for "strangers," the more friends and homies we get?

Oh, and by the way, I'm not a great ping-pong player, and I'm a fairly good driver!

Breaking Bad Mental Models

To help you minimize drawing inaccurate conclusions based on long-standing mental models, here are some questions to ask, an activity, and an assignment for this week.

1. **First glance.** What mental models of people exist in your organization? What effects could these models possibly have?

2. **Looking inward.** What mental models about people exist in your brain? How did they get there? How do they influence your interactions with others?

3. **What if?** What if you could change your mental models and have complete control over their reconstruction? What mental models would you tackle and how would you change them?

4. **Activity.** In a small group, discuss how mental models were built into you and how they may have had a negative impact on you and others.

5. **This week's assignment.** Pick a mental model of people you would like to change. Make a conscious, intentional effort to change it. What would/could you do to change it?

| 16 |

Strange New Worlds

Can you name a 1960s television series that was one of the first programs to receive recognition for its diversity? If you said the original *Star Trek*, you're right. In many ways *Star Trek* went where no show had gone before.

Picture for a moment the crew on the bridge of the USS *Enterprise* in that early show. Do you notice the racial and ethnic diversity? Behind the captain's chair to the right is Lieutenant Uhura wearing her little earphone, instant-messaging other Starfleet ships. Toward the front sits Ensign Chekov, navigating the *Enterprise* to strange new worlds. Can you see Lieutenant Sulu? He is doing something technical, I'm sure.

Then, of course, there is the big cheese himself, Captain James T. Kirk, perched in his chair, looking at the vast screen before him. You know he's wondering when he will get his next chance to break Starfleet's Prime Directive. And next to him is Spock, a Vulcan, who seals the deal. You know you have diversity when you have someone from another planet on the crew.

Scurrying around the engine room is chief engineer "Scotty," working to squeeze just a little more speed out of the dilithium crystals, hoping the engine won't blow. And "Bones" (Dr. McCoy) is in the sick bay rehearsing another reason to tell Kirk, "Dammit, Jim, I'm only a doctor!"

It's easy to see why many saw *Star Trek* as a model of diversity. Some people might argue that the original *Star Trek* series outshines many modern shows with respect to racial and ethnic inclusion. However, a different perspective shows a different side of *Star Trek*. Let's examine the show through another lens—with an eye on hierarchy (read: power and distribution of privilege), from the top down.

What is the common characteristic of the captain (Kirk), the chief engineer (Scotty), and the chief medical officer (McCoy) of the *Enterprise*? If you are thinking, "they were white guys," you get it. Look closer. What about the first officer (Spock)? Yes, he was half alien, but his other half was … white guy!

So, from a hierarchical perspective, *Star Trek* was not diverse. The main characters on the show, the ones who got the most airtime, were rather homogeneous from a race or ethnicity perspective. In fact, as a friend of mine put it, half-jokingly, "*Star Trek* wasn't a show about diversity. It was just another show about a typical white guy sitting in a big easy chair watching a big-screen TV and telling people what to do." This does not mean that "white guys" are bad or that they should not be leaders. It is merely an observation. After my friend shared his perspective with me, I saw what he saw, understood what he meant. But I quickly asked him if he could sit down and have a drink with a person who sees the show from the "diverse" perspective, if he could be friends with that person. I told him I wanted to live in a world where people who see the world differently can still come together to seek a common good, to find mutual benefit.

How Well Do You Engage Different Perspectives?

If you laughed a little at my friend's comment, you are well on your way to attaining a key ingredient in the stew of creativity and innovation: openness to different perspectives. Let me be clear that being open to different perspectives does not mean you must accept them. It simply means you are willing to entertain and understand a perspective that differs from yours. If you didn't laugh at my friend's joke, well, you are the very person for whom this book was written.

Humor aside, these two ways of looking at *Star Trek* illustrate how people with different perspectives can view the same set of "facts" and come away with very different interpretations. Neither is necessarily right or wrong; each interpretation is valid from a particular perspective, using a particular lens. The problem is that there are often multiple valid perspectives, but not enough people are willing to consider perspectives that don't fit comfortably within their limited framework of reality.

We are constantly interpreting information. And we base our interpretations on a set of lenses generated by our past encounters and experiences. A definition of culture by sociologist James Spradley underscores this simply and succinctly: "Culture is the acquired knowledge people use to interpret experience and generate behavior." It is not a big stretch to understand how different people, with their different experiences, can interpret the same information quite differently.

The existence of different perspectives and interpretations is not necessarily good or bad. However, we run into problems when we convince ourselves that our interpretation, our perspective, is the correct one, and that all others are flawed. "We must be right," we tell ourselves! But our tunnel vision often blinds us to opportunities literally sitting in our midst, made invisible by our inflexible worldview. When we are unwilling to hear or experience others' views, we lose the potential richness of multiple, diverse perspectives. We rob ourselves of possible solutions to vexing problems.

How tolerant are you of different perspectives? How willing are you to look through another lens? Your openness to considering different ideas, especially those that might initially make you uncomfortable, has a direct impact on how you operate in an increasingly diverse world, where multiple approaches, ideas, and ways of doing things are vital to long-term success.

So go ahead—take a voyage to explore strange new worlds. Make it your ongoing mission to boldly go to places you have never gone before. Break the Prime Directive and get involved in the lives of those you found alien in the past. It may be uncomfortable, even painful for a time. But after a while you most likely will enjoy your journey. If you allow it to, the journey will transform your thinking. It will bring out a new you—an open-minded person with the courage to entertain the exciting unpredictability that novelty brings. And imagine what might happen if the starship, uh, organization you are in were filled with people like that. The possibilities are endless. Ready to turn on the warp drive? Then, engage! And live long and prosper, my friend.

Who's on Your Bridge?

To help you begin to evaluate your cultural lenses and filters and entertain new perspectives, here are some questions to ask, an activity, and an assignment for this week.

1. **First glance.** What does the "bridge" of your organization's starship look like? How might your colleagues view it?

2. **Looking inward.** How do you see the starship *Enterprise*? Do you see it as a model for diversity, or a continuation of the "same old, same old"? How strongly do you stick to your interpretation of facts in the face of other perspectives? Are you able to entertain the possibility that a different interpretation also may be accurate?

3. **What if?** What if you walked through your organization trying to see it from the perspective of a colleague who is, in some ways, very different from you? What might you notice that would be cause for deeper consideration?

4. **Activity.** Using a flip chart to record your observations, examine the bridge of your organization, work group, or office. How do you see your company doing in respect to diversity? Do persons of color and women (as examples) span all levels in your organization? Identify three or four concrete actions your group could take to help fill the gaps on your bridge. Discuss some ways you might increase the number of multiple, diverse perspectives in leadership, in decision making, in development, and so on.

Who's on Your Bridge? (cont'd)

5. **This week's assignment.** Walk through your neighborhood and view it from the perspective of a small child, a person from a different socioeconomic class or racial background from yours, an individual who is less or more physically able than you, someone with a different sexual orientation from yours, a person who speaks English better or worse than you, and so on. Practice seeing the world through a different set of lenses.

| 17 |
Man 2.0

I did it. I quit. I've torn up my Man Card and canceled my membership in the Distinguished Alliance of Male Networkers, or DAMN for short. Didn't know such a thing existed, did you? It seemed like such a good deal for a long time, but as I grew older, I became aware of some unintended consequences resulting from my membership in DAMN. Members of DAMN are generally good, caring guys (and I mean guys, with the XY chromosome pair). The vast majority of them are caring and well intentioned. I still have DAMN friends. But like everyone else, many of my buddies and I in the DAMN club have blind spots, especially in relation to XX chromosome–defined beings.

Here's my story. I've been a DAMN member most of my adult life, though my recruitment began as a child. From my earliest memories, I recall subtle and overt messages that alluded to the many benefits that awaited me upon my entry into DAMN. As a DAMN member, I was told I would have special privileges, like not having to wait in line to use the bathroom. I would never be asked to get coffee at a meeting. Taking notes in a meeting is not expected of those privileged to be in DAMN, and members are precluded from doing yard work unless it involves a high-horsepower combustible engine. The DAMN membership pamphlet promised that non-DAMN members (i.e., women) would take care of those and other related tasks. *Cool*, I thought as a 10-year-old.

At my first DAMN meeting, held at a golf course, which by the way is the preferred venue for member meetings, I was given the DAMN Handbook. It was our daily guidebook and operations manual. Developed over many centuries by macho, testosterone-filled men, no others were to see the secrets between the covers of the handbook except DAMN members. Filled with wonderful advice, it guided my entry into adult life. Especially helpful, so I once thought, were the Five DAMN Commandments:

DAMN members shall...

1) Be aggressive and tough. Emotions shall not be displayed, as they are a clear signal of weakness. Exception: Members can show emotions if there is a ball around. For example, if there is a football, soccer ball, basketball, baseball, or puck (if you reside in Canada) within 100 yards, DAMN members can laugh, cry, hug, even kiss (but only on the forehead), and pat one another on their rears. Exception to the Exception: Volleyballs only count when men are playing, and ping-pong balls definitely do not count.

2) Compete and win at all costs. Competition shall be seen as an outcome-oriented endeavor. There shall always be a winner and a loser (sometimes many losers). The person in second place shall be deemed the first loser. No DAMN member shall

compete in events in which EVERYONE receives a ribbon, trophy, medal, or any other shiny object merely for participating.

3) Always speak in the language of sports and sports analogies. At least once a day, DAMN members are to reference sports and/or use sports phrases in conversation with others. Examples of appropriate references are, "He hit a home run with that idea," and, "There are no mulligans with this client." Ping-pong references and phrases do not count.

4) Know only seven colors, plus or minus two. The core colors being red, green, blue, yellow, gray, black, and white. Colors shall not have adjectives in front of them, as in "forest green." Exception: Adjectives indicating "degree" may be used, as in "light blue" or "dark red." Another Exception: Certain adjectives used to describe exquisite automobiles are allowed, as in "candy apple red."

5) Never ask for directions. Enough said.

In addition to the Five DAMN Commandments, my DAMN Handbook described special privileges afforded to members in good standing. For example, I would only need a small vocabulary of words (approximately 200) because members of DAMN are men of action. Talk is weak. We're DOERS! We fix problems. And when no problems exist, we have an inherent right to create problems so we can fix them—you know, be MEN! Long ago when DAMN members fixed something, they got to grunt and beat their chests. Today, members get designated parking spots near their corner office, and are allowed to text and act disinterested in meetings, especially when non-DAMN members are speaking.

DAMN members are excused from listening to anyone who begins conversations with things like, "So what do you all think about that...?" or, "How do you feel right now?" and, "Let's play ping-pong." Moreover, it's perfectly permissible (and even expected) to talk over another person. Members are not required to wait until others are finished with their sentence or thought before providing comments. Members can have side conversations whenever they wish and not care about how others feel about it. DAMN ideas have top priority.

Our motto? You guessed it—"DAMN it!" It's used whenever anything goes wrong and imparts blame on someone else. For instance, if I'm at a party and I somehow spill my drink, I am expected to exclaim, "Damn it!" and glare at someone, anyone, nearby. Another example: a member will shout "DAMN it!" if such member finds himself in a car accident. However, it must only be said when he gets out of the car and others are around to be blamed, not immediately after impact when he is all by himself in the car.

The DAMN Handbook is filled with lots of stuff like that. I loved that book when I became a member, but over time, it didn't seem right to do the things it suggested and even required. It didn't seem fair to blame someone else when I was at fault. It didn't seem fully healthy to disregard and downplay the importance of things like empathy, caring, and mindfulness of others—stuff the DAMN handbook called "touchy-feely" and "warm and fuzzy." I began to recognize that being a member of DAMN required me, in many ways, to be only half-human at times (maybe not even that much). In fact, over the course of many years, I've come to see that some things that were required of me and other card-carrying DAMN members didn't square well with my sense of right and wrong. It certainly didn't align well with my belief that nonmembers (women and others) are just as capable, talented, and valuable as any DAMN member, especially in our modern world, where the Alpha is no longer the most physically strong. No, today's Apex predator will have to have some attributes that the DAMN Handbook overlooked.

What pushed me over the cliff to help me recognize the potential harm of the expectations and requirements of DAMN membership? Two words—My Children. I do my three sons (Nicholas, Zachary, and Jacob) a disservice if I model to them the old, worn-out ways of what some call "masculine behavior"—a model that, in many ways, prevents men from accessing half of their humanness. Such a model overemphasizes things like aggressiveness, emotionless action (NOTE: humanly impossible), and physical prowess while underemphasizing things like emotional well-being, empathy, and communication and relational skills. And I do my daughter much harm if I, in some way, signal to her that girls and women are second-class citizens who are not worthy of the privileges and benefits that we men have given ourselves for many, many years. Indeed, until we men acknowledge the fact that we have "male privilege," we will not have the privilege of being the best dad, partner, husband, leader that we are capable of becoming.

Are all men DAMN members? Of course not, but my work takes me to environments where I encounter many men who still operate under a twentieth-century (and earlier) male model—a model that urgently needs a twenty-first-century makeover. And unfortunately, many of those men are in leadership positions. Fortunately, I have also come across many men who do not ascribe to the tenets of the DAMN Handbook and understand that a twenty-first-century world will require men (and women) who have a balanced combination of what many think of as feminine and masculine attributes. Denying the former or the latter attributes results in an incomplete human being.

Man 1.0 is dead. My Man Card is torn up. Long live Man 2.0. That said, I still find it difficult to ask for driving directions. Old habits are hard to break.

Becoming Fully Human

To help you become a more "whole" person, here are some questions to ask, an activity, and an assignment for this week.

1. **First glance.** What are some things your organization can do to help everyone better understand their deficits and become more "fully human" as it relates to understanding others?

2. **Looking inward.** Take a critical look at what you've been taught. What areas might need to be transformed to help you become a better person in a global society?

3. **What if?** What if you could, in a snap, change an aspect of yourself that could help you relate to people better? What would you change?

4. **Activity.** In a small group, have each individual share what they came up with in question 3 above.

5. **This week's assignment.** Pick an area of your life that could use a metamorphosis for the better. Draw up a practice plan that could help you transform yourself for the better, then PRACTICE!

| 18 |

I Know Everything Already

Several years ago I was teaching a freshman-level class on critical inquiry and expression. Among other things, the course required students to explore their world with a critical eye focused through a lens of multiculturalism.

One of the first assignments was for the students to write a short paper about an experience that had taught them something significant. There was great variety in the quality of the finished products, with many of the papers well written and others…let's just say I ran out of ink marking them up.

Several of the papers are still clear in my memory, not because they were terrific but because they illustrated some of the ways in which first-year students' brains are hardwired. The paper that taught me the most was one submitted by a young woman. I don't remember exactly what she wrote about, but the story involved a football game and a corsage made of chrysanthemums—you know, pom-poms.

I recall that I wrote a lot on this particular paper. What struck me most were all the times I had to circle spelling errors, mainly the misspelling of *pom-poms*, which the young woman had spelled with an *n*, as in *pom-pons*.

Shortly after I returned the papers to the class, the student who had written the "pom-pons" paper approached me. She pointed to all the times I had circled *pom-pons* and asked, "What's wrong with that?" I told her that the word was misspelled, and she countered that *pom-pons* was a correct alternate (read: "diverse") spelling.

"How dare she argue with me," I thought. Doesn't she know that the three letters following my name, PhD, make me an expert—about everything, including the spelling of *pom-poms*? Obviously, she couldn't care less about the PhD that I had worked so hard to get. I could have had MA, BA, ESPN, NBC, CNN, SBC, AAA, or NBA after my name. To her, the letters might make me an expert in some areas, but not in flowers. She probably was thinking there should be a four-letter word following my name.

As she continued to protest, I dug in deeper. My pom-pom fortress would not crumble or crack, especially under pressure from this bothersome freshman gnat. Didn't she know that I had won my district's spelling bee as a third-grader? As I tried to shoo her away, she reached into her book bag. Thoughts flashed through my mind about psycho students who shoot their professors over a poor grade. Could this be about to happen? After fumbling in her bag for what seemed like minutes, she drew her weapon. "Here's a dictionary. Look it up if you don't believe me."

With great confidence, I began paging through the book, all the while picturing her forthcoming apology for questioning me. "There," I said, "it's *pom-pom*."

She looked at me with surprise. "Are you sure?"

Just to appease her, I pointed to the word and said, "See for yourself."

She looked more closely at the dictionary, then eyed me with disgust. "According to this dictionary, another correct spelling is *pom*-pon."

I looked again. She was right. It could be spelled with an *n*. Though the evidence was right there in front of me, I didn't want to believe it. "Must be a mistake," I thought. How could I be wrong? Had the young woman published her own dictionary in her quest for a better grade? Although I wasn't 100 percent convinced, I told the student I would reassess her paper. And I went back to my office to check my own dictionary. It, too, had the "wrong" spelling as an alternative.

My certainty was shaken by this young whippersnapper, who basically had told me, "Hey, stupid, the world is round, not flat!" In the end, I had to admit that I was wrong. The world is indeed round. In wondering about how I could have been wrong all those years, I realized that I had never in my life heard anyone say *pom-pon*. I had only heard the word pronounced *pom-pom*. Maybe someone has said *pom-pon* to me, but I filtered it into *pom-pom*. People who had "taught" me didn't include an alternate possibility and passed their narrow view on to me.

What Are You Misspelling?

"You don't know what you don't know." I'm sure you've heard that saying before. It certainly makes sense that you can't know something of which you have no knowledge. The problem is that often we *think* we know more than we actually do. Or, worse, we believe that the limited knowledge we have about something is comprehensive and, moreover, that it's absolutely true. When challenged, we resist the notion that we could be wrong. "It can't be that way," we say to ourselves. "That's not what I learned."

In that embarrassing story about the pom-pons is a lesson about the need to emphasize our curiosity about the world and other people while minimizing our certainty about things we think we know. There is also a lesson about how ignorance and arrogance make a formidable duo that prevents us from exploring new perspectives and ideas.

When it comes to our ideas about people, is it possible that we hold information that we believe to be true when in fact it's greatly distorted? Could it be that we live sheltered from people who are different from us, which has led us to believe "pom-poms" about others when in fact the reality could easily be "pom-pons"?

The natural thing for us to do when our world is being challenged is defend our turf. On gender issues, I've heard more than once, "We don't have any women in leadership positions, but we aren't sexist. Everyone here has the same opportunities." Then, when challenged further, we come up with a great rationalization for our position: "Women just haven't been in the workplace as long as men," as if every man in leadership has worked a long time to achieve that position. It couldn't be true that males have developed a structure and network that, for the most part, hinders the advancement of women. We tell women that they just need to work harder. Or we tell them not to have kids, or that they are too emotional and read too much into things. Nope, it couldn't be that the "real" world is a little different from the tidy little world we have in our mind. After all, it's *pom-poms*, right?

That incident taught me that some parts, potentially many parts, of my knowledge base might have faulty data, that I may have been given bad information throughout my life. That realization is tough to accept because it forces me to question much of the information I have about my world. I have to start asking myself, "Where did I learn that? Was the source credible? Have I been exposed to different perspectives? Am I too arrogant to admit that I could be wrong, or that I am wrong? Am I willing to step out of my comfort zone to grow?" In an age of technology, when we have access to many types of information from myriad sources, we often still gravitate to what is familiar, to what "speaks our language" and doesn't challenge us much. And therein lies the trap: Our quest for comfort and stability makes us defensive in the face of new and different ideas.

So how will you and your organization react when the "new" and the "different" are no longer easily ignored? Will you open up to other possibilities, though it may initially cause embarrassment or even pain? Or will you be like the fifteenth- and sixteenth-century leaders who stood by their position even in the face of evidence that Earth revolves around the sun, not the other way around?

My challenge to those of us who tend to be certain about our world is this: Minimize certainty and maximize curiosity, especially when it comes to people and ideas with which we have very little interaction. There is much to learn from being more curious.

By the way, are you supposed to capitalize *pom-pons*?

Learning How to Spell

Perhaps it's time to correct or expand some comfortable "spelling" assumptions. To help guide you through this process, here are some questions to ask, an activity, and an assignment for this week.

1. **First glance.** Is it possible that you have some "pom-poms" (i.e., misconceptions) in your mental makeup? What pom-poms are in your organization?

2. **Looking inward.** Are you on a quest for comfort or curiosity? Are you willing to step out of your pom-poms world and humble enough to face some uncertainty? Are you willing to entertain a pom-*pons* reality—with an open mind and a humble spirit?

3. **What if?** What if our accumulated knowledge has more pom-poms than pom-*pons*? What if what we've been taught is a "flat world" view of a round world?

4. **Activity.** Discuss a situation similar to the one in this story when you had to correct what you previously had thought to be true. How devastating, really, was the outcome? What did you learn?

5. **This week's assignment.** Shake off some old pom-poms beliefs. Think about something that you hold to be true but others have disagreed with. Ask yourself whether your position is based on empirical evidence or on personal preference—maybe something you accepted with little critical examination or thought. Stretch yourself beyond your comfort zone.

| 19 |

Our Ongoing Mission

Every once in a while, I painfully discover black holes in my belief system. For example, in my youth I believed expiration dates on food items were to be ignored, that they were planned obsolescence ploys to get one to purchase more food. No longer. I used to think it wise to wash clothes of all colors and materials in one load. Nowadays, not so much. I previously thought it perfectly normal to vocally express outrage toward so-called "officials" for bad calls at my kids' sporting events. No more.

On these epiphanic occasions, my ancient brain's reactionary response is, in Star Trek terms, "Shields up!" Yes, encounters with information that challenges long-standing beliefs raise my cognitive "shields" and place my brain's neurons on red alert. In the face of conflicting information, I stubbornly cling to my position. Even when I encounter a position I can't find holes in or evidence I can't refute, I find myself to be a good "cling-on." After all, in my universe, I am always right.

In a twenty-first-century world, we encounter terabytes of information each time we turn on a television, pick up a newspaper, or log on to

Facebook. Our brains are perpetually processing information, assessing the data for its validity and value. Though we often attempt to put ourselves in comfortable environments where the information aligns with what we have in our head, invariably we're hit with external pieces of the data puzzle that do not fit with the internal picture created in our minds. These occasions have a name. Researchers call this "cognitive dissonance."

We don't like cognitive dissonance. In fact, our brain finds it rather uncomfortable and attempts to warp-drive out of it very quickly. When people enter my sector of space and challenge my notions of the galaxy—in effect suggesting that I might be wrong—I have a choice to make in order to reduce or eliminate my dissonance: Do I entertain their ideas (potentially learning something), OR do I stick to my beliefs (protecting my understanding of the galaxy)? Would it surprise you to find out that all of us have a cognitive bias toward the latter?

Why do we find opposing beliefs so challenging? Why is it so difficult for us to even consider that something might be awry in our belief system? From a psychological perspective, discovering we might be wrong about one thing forces us to consider that we might be wrong about other things. If one belief domino falls, what others must follow? The very prospect of being mistaken, especially with what we consider to be foundational or long-standing beliefs, is psychologically troubling. So, rather than reexamining and reevaluating the things we *know* to be true, the mentally easier thing to do is simply reject or ignore the dissonance-producing information—better to be comfortable with long-held beliefs than to wrestle with the discomfort of having to adopt new, strange ones. The problem is that our long-accepted beliefs may have been built on a shaky foundation.

Indeed, research suggests we have a great bias for believing that our perspectives and ideas are absolutely correct. Which makes logical sense, because why would we hold on to a belief when we know it is false? Moreover, we tend to *think* we know more than we actually do. It has a lot to do with our brain's dislike of uncertainty and ambiguity, so we create stories of certainty that we must rationalize. Therein lies a big issue…we sometimes get things wrong and we often forget our perspective is just one of myriad valid perspectives. The reality is that we only have a relatively small slice of the information pie. None of us has complete knowledge of our world. None of us holds all perspectives, all data, and all available information. Now consider that we form conclusions and make judgments about right and wrong based on data coming from narrow sets of experiences and a constrained knowledge base. If that foundation is inherently limited, it is not a big cognitive leap to conclude that our views of the world, of people, of ideas, are also limited. Not necessarily wrong, but necessarily limited.

If this last paragraph hasn't cause you too much cognitive dissonance and you're still psychologically *with me*, then you just might have the mental makeup to be a paragon citizen in a twenty-first-century world filled with differences. A world in which people with visible tattoos are both wrong…and right. (Say what?) A world where one can disagree with another's view on sexual orientation and still have laughs at dinner together. (Say again?) Maybe even a world in which a Michigan State Spartan dad will pay for his son to attend the University of Michigan. (No way!) In such a world, it is useful to remind ourselves that encounters with different people are essentially encounters with different viewpoints—not necessarily right or wrong, just different.

What does this all mean for us who value, or *say* we value, inclusion and diversity? One thing it means is that we must be mindful of not equating different with wrong or bad. It is something our brain has a tendency to do. Tendencies are changeable. However, as with anything else that is changeable, actual change requires effort, sometimes even a lot of effort over many years. I've been trying to get my wife to leave the toilet seat up for the better part of 20 years. I can report no change as of yet. Another thing it means is that we should expect cognitive dissonance in a world filled with differences. To get the most out of those uncomfortable encounters, we should practice reframing states of dissonance as opportunities to learn.

For me, I've come to learn and fully realize that others' perspectives are often just one of many valid perspectives that can coexist. To get to that learning outcome, I've practiced being mindful of asking myself a few questions as I encounter opposing, dissonance-producing viewpoints. The first question I ask is, "What path might the other person have walked that led them to that conclusion?" Then I ask a second, similar question, "What path did I walk that led me to my conclusion?" Finally, I ask why I hold some beliefs—beliefs that I cannot empirically prove—with absolute certainty. By practicing asking and answering these questions, I am essentially taking down my cognitive shields and entertaining others' perspectives without judgment of right and wrong. What I am doing is building my muscle for curiosity and open-mindedness, a muscle necessary for the heavy lifting required for those who value inclusion and diversity. It is this muscle that allows me to entertain multiple perspectives beyond my own, and when I can do that well, I give myself more opportunities to learn and to become, hopefully, a little wiser.

In a dynamic twenty-first-century world, filled with turbulence and rapid change, we would be wise to be more curious and open-minded. We would do well to adopt *Star Trek*'s theme of exploring, of getting beyond our own comfortable spaces. Again, be mindful that as you break the gravitational pull of comfort you will invariably experience cognitive dissonance. Sometimes a little. Sometimes a lot. A "shields up" approach to dissonance, while sometimes helpful, can also be very limiting. If we have the courage to lower our shields and challenge default answers and comfortable patterns, we just might discover that strange others and their strange beliefs are only strange because we've spent little or no time with them. If we make it our ongoing mission to explore "strange new worlds" (and the creatures we come upon), we might be surprised at how exciting, educational, and enjoyable the voyage can be.

In many ways, the twenty-first-century experience is all about strange, otherworldly encounters. As members of a dynamic, global community, we have the opportunity to constantly engage with a host of diverse perspectives. An ability to entertain myriad perspectives and reframe them as opportunities for learning will raise the probability of positive outcomes. So lower your shields. Become explorers of outer spaces as well as your own inner mental spaces. Challenge yourself to grapple with seemingly strange ideas with the goal of understanding without judgment. If you allow it, the journey will transform your thinking, a metamorphosis of the mind, if you will. What can emerge is a more curious, open-minded person with the motivation and courage to break the boundaries of comfort zones. It is beyond these familiar mental and physical spaces where serotonin-producing "Ahas" take place. Your voyage will not always be easy. You will encounter aliens with, well, alien ideas. You will encounter cultures that will disrupt your conventions. But make no mistake; your efforts will open you to a world of never-before-seen possibilities and opportunities.

Ready to turn on your warp drive for an exciting journey that can propel you to new discoveries about self, others, and the world? Then, engage! And live long and prosper, my fellow explorers.

Explore Strange New Worlds

To help you become more mindful of venturing out of your comfort zones and environments of familiarity, here are some questions to ask, an activity, and an assignment for this week.

1. **First glance.** What are some organizational beliefs that people hold that should probably be jettisoned?

2. **Looking inward.** Think about how you've handled cognitive dissonance in the past. What are some good examples of how you handled it? What are some negative examples?

3. **What if?** What if you handled cognitive dissonance in a more positive manner? What would that look like?

4. **Activity.** In a small group, discuss how cognitive dissonance could be used to the organization's advantage.

5. **This week's assignment.** Practice becoming more aware of what causes cognitive dissonance. How might this be helpful as you relate to others and their different ideas, values, and beliefs?

| 20 |

Simple Naked Singularities

"It's pretty simple," my son Nicholas matter-of-factly said as he explained the concept of naked singularities. I don't remember much else of the conversation except words like "black hole" and "sucked." And before your mind goes too deeply into the gutter, a naked singularity is a space-time phenomenon, not something out of a middle school sex-ed class. Oh, I also remember pondering if I was smarter than an eighth grader (bet a similar thought is bouncing in your head right now as well).

What struck me as my son talked, was his use of the word "simple" in explaining something that defies Einstein's Theory of Relativity. Indeed, he made the phenomenon sound simple, though I suspect it is much more complex. He probably thought his old man's brain would disintegrate into a dust pile if he went into any more detail. He was probably right. When it comes to naked singularities, simple will do.

Like most people, I prefer simple over complex. "Simple" is easier than "complex." Sounds better, too. Ever heard of a music group called

Complex Minds or a magazine named *Complexity*? Didn't think so. *Simple Minds* and *Simplicity* are much more inviting-sounding names. There's no getting around it, we human creatures like simple. We like it so much we created this thing called the "KISS" principle—Keep It Simple, Stupid! Soothingly succinct, the KISS principle reduces a shades-of-gray world to the simplicity of black and white, right and wrong.

But what if, and pardon me as I suggest such a ridiculous notion, the world in which we operate is rather complex. No really, stay with me here. Could it be mind-meltingly true that complex environments and issues are more prevalent than we desire? And what happens if we attempt to apply the KISS principle under the condition of complexity? Well, let's take a look.

First, we must define this thing called "complexity." Complexity can be defined as a situation in which one has many variables to consider, and that these variables interact in often unpredictable ways. Other things being equal, an environment with 10 variables is more complex than one with three variables. For example, if you have three playing cards, there is a total of six different ways you can combine the cards ($3 \times 2 \times 1 = 6$). If you have 10 cards, then the possible combinations is 3,628,800 ($10 \times 9 \times 8 \times 7 \times 6 \times 5 \times 4 \times 3 \times 2 \times 1 = 3,628,800$). Think about how complex it might be if you have 100 or 1,000 variables. Get the picture of complexity? With that said, let's look at how we operationalize the KISS principle, or, *Keep It Simple Stupid*, a concept introduced by US Navy engineers.

To apply the KISS principle (to simplify) means that one must purge some variables. Well, guess which variables we tend to discard? Often it's the ones we don't understand well. Or the ones that cause us much angst. Sometimes we get rid of variables that do not fit with our perceived reality or mental models. There's nothing necessarily wrong with eliminating variables—unless those variables we are tossing out are crucial to understanding the problem and finding a solution.

For example, what if achieving success requires more than just working hard? Of course, we all know success (defined in this case from a capitalistic perspective) is the result of a combination of factors, some of which are not directly under our control. For example, having connections can help a great deal in one's success. Think of the saying "It's who you know." Having money at your disposal is often beneficial. Hard to "self-actualize" when you're scrounging for food and shelter. Knowing the right people and having money are powerful factors that could potentially lead to success. I bet many factors are involved in the equation for success. Being in the right place at the right time probably doesn't hurt. Being appropriately tall or short has its place. Studies suggest that being considered attractive is attractive to those you would like to attract in your quest for success. Being born in a certain time period, or in a particular geographic region or country, can also be factors that can influence one's potential success. The list of factors is long.

But somehow, some folks have taken that long list of potential "success" factors, applied the KISS principle, and mindlessly reduced the list to one factor—hard work. These well-meaning people walk around saying things like, "You can be anything you want if you just work hard," or they'll tell others to "pull yourself up by your own bootstraps." The ones who read the Christian Bible might even offer up this one to put the final nail into the coffin: "Idle hands are the work of the devil."

While the message of hard work embedded in these sayings is certainly a positive one, there is a danger in reducing the many factors that can potentially lead to success down to one—because if hard work is the lone factor that leads to success, then the lack of hard work (laziness) must certainly be the cause of failure. And here's the trap door that leads to unintentional intolerance. Once we put the "lazy" label on someone or some group, we tend not to be compassionate, understanding, or helpful toward that person or group.

We have framed laziness as a conscious choice people make, and as such we look negatively upon lazy people (because it's their choice to be couch potatoes). We don't help lazy people. We help those who work hard. In a sense, we let ourselves off the hook of having to help others, especially others who are strangers to us—the people of stereotypes. We may have some degree of cognitive dissonance (guilt) if we don't have compassion for and assist those who do not find success because of reasons beyond their control.

No such dissonance torments us if we can label people as slackers who have "chosen" not to walk the road of success—a road fully paved with the blood, sweat, and tears of hard work. The nonbiblical quote often attributed to the Bible used by some when confronted with lazy people is "God helps those who help themselves."

Before anyone misinterprets what I am saying, I want to make it clear that I believe in the importance of "hard work," that it is often a necessary ingredient in the recipe for success. But it is usually only one of many. And research suggests the biggest factor is randomness, or pure luck. Consider that no one got to choose what family they were born into. I also want to make it crystal clear that a culture that places great value on "individual choice" and romanticizes the Horatio Alger story can lead individuals within that culture to peel the many layers of the success onion down to one single layer—HARD WORK. And then the blaming and negative comments about "those lazy people" emerge. "If only they would work harder," the mindless chorus sings.

I suspect that mostly everyone in a mindful, reflective state will agree that hard work is just one of myriad factors—some within and others outside our control—that contribute to success. The problem is, as cognitive researchers suggest, we are often mindless, and in our mindlessness, our brain efficiently uses our past experiences and acquired knowledge about others to make quick, superficial judgments. This can lead to errors in judgment and errors in "labeling" when we lack sufficient information about a person or situation. Recall that our brain works on an efficiency principle and therefore takes shortcuts whenever it can as a way of conserving precious energy. It can conserve more energy by reducing the number of factors it must consider in making calculations of a situation. Our brain loves the KISS principle.

So, what are we to do to reduce potential mistakes in labeling others? First, we must recognize that we all label others using categories and mental models developed through previous experiences. Recognizing this natural brain operation is key. Second, remember that our brain, as a means of conserving energy, takes shortcuts and simplifies our world for us. Put differently, it minimizes the number of variables it must calculate in any situation. Third, in its desire to simplify, it sometimes discards valuable variables and factors (or does not even perceive them in the first place), potentially leading to mistakes in judgment, perception, and interpretation. Our brain tends to filter out any information that might cause more neurons to go online. This partially explains why we gravitate toward people and ideas that fit our conception of the world and reject other things that do not conform to our mental models. This is the KISS principle in action.

Wow, it almost seems as if there is not much we can do to better the situation if our brain operates with its own KISS principle. But there are some things we can do to break from the gravitational pull of simplicity and closed-mindedness. One important action step is to become more aware and mindful of when we are simplifying too much and leaving out important, crucial information.

It will be difficult, but we can put down our "smart" phones and other attention-grabbing gadgets in order to listen more intently to differing points of view. We might even take it a step further by asking ourselves what different conclusions we might draw if we took other perspectives into account. Stop texting and checking your email every five minutes. I'm pretty sure it won't kill you to do so, and I'm fairly confident it will make others in the room more appreciative.

We can surround ourselves more often with people who "force" us to consider other factors—factors we would normally not entertain. So, hang out with different people during lunch. Challenging ourselves to move out of our comfort zones and into the comfort zones of others gives us crucial practice in encountering a complex world.

All these things allow us to practice engaging complexity, and not oversimplifying when we do so. They allow us to experience "other" variables and factors so that we can become more comfortable with the new, novel, and different. To get better, we must practice what we want to get better at. It's really that simple (so to speak)! And it doesn't even have to involve naked singularities.

Examine How You KISS

To help you become more mindful of not oversimplifying, here are some questions to ask, an activity, and an assignment for this week.

1. **First glance.** How has simplifying helped and/or hurt your organization as you address issues of inclusion and diversity?

2. **Looking inward.** Examine how you think about complex aspects of your world. How has your brain oversimplified these aspects? What might be the consequences of oversimplifying them?

3. **What if?** What if where you are in life is an outcome of complex variables? What might those many variables be? What might happen if we were to discard crucial variables in our attempt to understand others and where they are in life?

4. **Activity.** In a small group, discuss how the application of the KISS principle has impacted hiring and promotions?

5. **This week's assignment.** Practice being more mindful of how your brain might oversimplify people in its attempt to understand others. Is there a pattern for whom you tend to oversimplify and how you go about oversimplifying them?

| 21 |

Someday They Will See

Imagine that you live in a community in which a small percentage of the population upholds the Christian faith. You are "one of those Christians." Your forefathers founded this community many generations ago, but over the course of time non-Christians "took over" and became the majority.

A few years ago the majority, the non-Christians, started a school. To honor those who had first settled the community, they decided to have as the school's team name "the Christians." Now, they never consulted Christians in the community about naming the team. They didn't even talk with anyone about how best to honor the community's founding fathers.

This majority doesn't know much about the Christian faith. They know that nearly all Christians participate in something called Communion on a regular basis, and they have observed the Communion process of eating bread and drinking wine. The majority have also noticed that Christian art often portrays someone hanging on a cross and that many Christians enact something called the Crucifixion at a time called Easter.

Now the majority has decided that the school's mascot should do something at school assemblies and athletic competitions to build school and community pride. Because the team is "the Christians," they think it should do something Christian-like, so they chose Communion as the perfect ritual to perform at school functions. Not only would it generate pride, they reason, but it also would show that Christians are valued in the community.

When you hear about the plan, you quickly suggest to the majority that what they are planning to do will not honor the Christian faith, but actually will dishonor it. You tell them that taking Communion is a sacred act of meaningful significance to Christians and that doing so for fun and show is blasphemous.

As you make your objections, many non-Christians become defensive. In fact, they take offense at your objections and insist that you should be thankful for their efforts to bring attention to a wonderful Christian ritual. You repeat your objections over and over, but the more you protest, the more they dig in their heels. Indeed, the more you object, the more they believe that what they are doing is an honoring gesture. They argue vehemently that they have good intentions and that you are taking this "Communion thing" way too seriously. They tell you to lighten up.

By this time, the reenactment of Communion has become a regular part of halftime activities at basketball and football games. People in the stands create motions around it, putting their hands to their mouth twice—to signify the eating of bread and the drinking of wine—when their team needs support. They've even added a life-sized cross with a real student tied to it for a "Crucifixion effect." Non-Christians in the community love it. They identify with it. They are full of school and community pride when they see it.

You and others in the Christian community continue to object. But because you are thought of as the minority, no one listens. Community and school leaders tell you to "get over it!" They continue to insist that there's nothing wrong with what they are doing and that they won't be bullied by "political correctness."

The heart of the Christian community sinks. Your defense of a significant act of faith has been deemed an act of political correctness. Though what they do inflicts pain on you and other Christians, you know that the majority don't know what they are doing. You forgive them in the midst of your pain, suffering, and humiliation. You go on. You learn to survive. You say to yourself and other Christians, "Someday they will see."

Doing the Honorable Thing

How much do you know about American Indians and their approach to spirituality and worship? If you don't know much, you might consider doing a little study. Maybe then you will see why the "mascot thing" is a big deal to many American Indians. Maybe you'll begin to understand that the issues go so beyond hurtful stereotypes that they touch on people's spirituality, religious rituals, and worldview. Imagine how you would feel if others made fun of your deeply held beliefs, then disregarded your pleas to stop. You might even begin to empathize with the argument that allowing a team in our national's capital to have an American Indian mascot borders on institutionalized racial prejudice (read: racism). That simple mascot thing turns out to be much more complex than many realize.

When we know little about others, about what they believe and value, we shouldn't be surprised when we make mistakes in our cross-cultural interactions, and yet we often are. Then, amazingly enough, as we stand like the proverbial deer in the headlights, we find ways to blame others, distancing ourselves from responsibility and relieving ourselves of culpability. How so? We tell others that they are being too sensitive. We accuse them of playing the race card. In our righteousness we recommend that they "pull themselves up by their bootstraps." In our arrogance we hold firm to our conviction that the playing field is level. Does any of this sound familiar?

A wise person once offered me some profound words, telling me, "Life is a game of error correction." But more profound were the challenging words that followed: "Are you humble enough to admit your mistakes and courageous enough to correct them?" Effectively engaging diversity and walking in the worlds of others requires well-meaning, compassionate, and fair-minded people to live mindfully, embrace humility, and act courageously. Are you up to the task, or is it just easier to believe that "those Indians" are making too big a deal out of that mascot thing?

Stepping into Moccasins

To help guide you through a more critical analysis of how to respect and honor those who may believe and do things a little (or a lot) differently from the way you do them, here are some questions to ask, an activity, and an assignment for this week.

1. **First glance.** What other examples of well-intentioned mascots, celebrations, or symbols can you think of that may need further exploration? How might we become more mindful and catch ourselves from inflicting unintentional pain on others?

2. **Looking inward.** Has anyone ever told you to quit being "so sensitive"? How did you feel?

3. **What if?** What if our uninformed acts of intended goodwill offend others? What if "just joking" isn't really funny to anyone but us? What if the honorable thing to do is not what you want to do?

4. **Activity.** Discuss some ways your organization may have attempted to honor cultures in the past without really learning about the issues or the historical and spiritual significance of traditions, symbols, or holidays. What are some ways your organization could honor and educate others around these cultural differences? Under what conditions might "celebrating" diversity turn out to be a bad thing?

5. **This week's assignment.** Ask people representing different traditions, customs, and beliefs in your organization to comment on a planned diversity-related activity and suggest ways to make it more sensitive to their culture and more meaningful.

| 22 |

A World of Mistakes

Every once in a while, I feel the need to confess that I make mistakes. In fact, I make numerous mistakes—just ask my family and friends, preferably when I'm in the vicinity. I would tell you about my blunders, but I'm afraid that if I turn on my spigot of slip-ups, I won't be able to shut it off. As an alternative, let me talk about other people's mistakes. Like many of you out there, I am pretty good at identifying the errors of others.

So I don't have people stalking me for pointing out their egregious errors, I'll begin with a mistake made by people who are no longer among the living. Here's one that might work: the world is flat. That's a doozy! How did the first people who may have pondered that issue arrive at this conclusion? Well, they just looked. One way of knowing is through observation, and long ago when our ancestors looked across the horizon, what they saw was pretty darn flat. It was hard to argue with this conclusion. You might say it was self-evident. But it was also wrong!

Yes, they were mistaken in their conclusion. How could they have been so, uh, well...stupid? Before we get all uppity with our ancestors and start ridiculing them for their simple-mindedness, let's show a little empathy and walk for a while along their path.

Let's do a mental exercise to try and get a glimpse of how our ancestors drew the conclusion of a flat Earth. Imagine you're outside in an open field. Now spin 360 degrees, and while you're spinning, make some observations about your world. Collect data. When finished with your spin and data collection, ask yourself what the observational data tell you. Based on the data you collected while getting dizzy, is the world flat or round? The data say **FLAT**, right?

As a budding scientist, you may say to me, "That's only one data point. We can't draw a conclusion from a sample size of one." I then ask you to mentally travel to other places to collect more data. I join you on this imaginary journey. We travel together to various locations around the world: China, South Africa, Egypt, Russia, France, and Brazil. In each place, after arriving and stepping off our imaginary plane, I ask you to do that 360-degree spin, make observations, and collect data. And in each place after your data collection, I ask you, "Based on your observational data, is the world flat or round?" What's your answer? All the data collected while making your observations tell you the world is **FLAT**— again and again and again, in each location, the observational data point to a flat Earth! But you and I both know the world is round or spherical. What are you missing that leads you to the wrong conclusion? You have empirical observational evidence that screams **FLAT**, yet that's flat-out wrong! How are you interpreting the data incorrectly? The problem is not that you are making interpretational mistakes of the data. It is clear that the data you collected say **FLAT**. The problem, at least in part, lies in the fact that you are missing other data sets coming from other perspectives.

What can we learn from this example? First, don't judge your ancestors before you walk in their footsteps. And second, when one is missing information, data, and perspectives, one can draw the wrong conclusion. Now let me ask you this: "Who out there knows everything, has all the information, data, and perspectives?" No human knows everything. All of us have incomplete knowledge when it comes to our world and the people and ideas in it. All of us are missing some data—a *lot* of data relative to the universe of data. And if that's the case, that we lack sufficient knowledge in many areas and subjects with which we have little experience, could we be wrong every once in a while, maybe *more* than every once in a while? I think you know the answer to that question.

What might increase our chances of being correct? The short answer is having more knowledge, data, and information, and specifically more knowledge and data from diverse sources (think diverse perspectives). Therein lies the power of diversity and the "wisdom of crowds." When it comes to problem solving (especially complex problem solving), we tip the odds in favor of discovering an optimal solution when we have diverse perspectives at our disposal. It's a simple matter of mathematical probability. Consider it this way: the more ideas and different perspectives you have, the greater the probability that one idea, or a combination of those ideas and perspectives, will provide the best solution.

The logic is straightforward. Ideas are the result of experiences and the birthplace of solutions (i.e., innovations). The more experiences one has individually and collectively, the greater the probability of discovering a solution. And it's not just having one or two individuals with diverse experiences—that's helpful. It's having many individuals representing a collective of diverse experiences—that's powerful!

Staying in our comfort zones and hanging out with people like ourselves contributes very little to building a diverse set of experiences and perspectives. Quite simply, if you believe that the world is flat, you're probably hanging out with people who believe that the world is flat. Hanging out with our "homies" is self- and group reinforcing, and it's a huge barrier to greater creativity; innovation; and, might I add, an inclusive and diverse environment.

Here's how it works. We tend to gravitate toward people and ideas that are similar to our own. Neuroscience research tells us our brain has a positive bias for familiarity and "comfort zones." Yes indeed, we find it very comfortable to surround ourselves with folks who think like us, act like us, look like us, and who generally share the same values and beliefs. These folks are our friends, our "homies." Besides being a great support group, our homies serve as a sounding board for us. They listen to what we have to say. And the vast majority of time, they agree with us, especially on important shared values. We need homies like this because they help us to navigate our world with some level of confidence. They serve as protective walls that shield us from weird and funny-sounding ideas.

Unfortunately, those same walls that can protect us also have the ability to imprison us. Indeed, our homies also serve to create walls that insulate us from ideas that, at times, we need to hear and critically entertain in order to solve problems and discover critical solutions. They prevent us from hearing and seeing alternatives to our current reality—alternatives that can only come from "outside" perspectives and sets of experiences different than our own. Within the comfortable "walls of sameness" we are unable to recognize or even see the "crucial" perspectives and data that could lead us to different possibilities and solutions. In the end, we see **FLAT** when the reality is **ROUND**.

Intentionally or unintentionally creating relative homogeneity (sameness) can easily prevent an organization from seeing things they need to see and considering things they need to consider. And that's a big mistake for any organization that seeks to be more creative and innovative.

I'd talk more about other people's mistakes, but I'm darn close to my

144

1,300-word limit for this piece. As we leave, let me suggest to you that 8 + 4 is 12, but it is also something else. What's your quick reaction? Before your mental model of Asians as math whizzes crumbles, let me remind you that there are multiple systems (bases) in which one can do math. Here's a parting word from a former coach of mine—"Life is a game of error correction." Are you humble enough to admit mistakes and courageous enough to correct them?

Practicing Minimizing Mistakes

To help you minimize drawing inaccurate conclusions based on limited data and information, here are some questions to ask, an activity, and an assignment for this week.

1. **First glance.** What "walls of sameness" exist in your organization? How have they been helpful? How have they been harmful?

2. **Looking inward.** When it comes to other people, what are some conclusions you draw from them that you think would change if you had other sets of data? How else can you get more data?

3. **What if?** What if you became less certain and more curious about ideas and beliefs about people that you have always held to be true? What might happen if you stepped out of your world of certainty to consider other ways you can think about people? For those who have a quick, uncomfortable reaction to this question, ask why.

4. **Activity.** In a small group, discuss some things about the workplace (whether it's people, ideas, and/or patterns of doing) of which people tend to be certain. In this discussion, ask what data, information, and/or perspectives might be missing that could lead to different ways of thinking and doing.

5. **This week's assignment.** Practice stepping out of your mental and physical comfort zones to discover missing information about things that you seem to be certain about. Challenge what you "know" to be true by having a conversation with people who could give you different insights.

| 23 |

Recording Errors

If you own a relatively new computer, the system you have probably allows you to write data onto a CD or a DVD. The computer I purchased several years ago has a nifty CD writer that lets me digitally record my favorite songs onto discs. Though I thought this was pretty cool technology when I bought the computer, I hadn't put it to use until recently.

It was a wonderfully calm Saturday afternoon at our house. I remember the calmness well because with four children all under age eight, this rare phenomenon occurs at Halley's Comet–like intervals. And it only happened this time because somehow the stars and moon aligned and all the kids were napping. I remember asking my wife to bottle whatever she had done to get them all simultaneously into a nearly comatose state. "Already did it," she joked, pointing to a newly purchased bottle of cough medicine on the counter. (No, we don't dope our kids.) But back to the calm afternoon.

I wanted to do something special with the few blessed hours of peace and quiet. So I got to work on something I had been wanting to do for years—make a CD of songs that would transport me romantically back to my younger days. Ahh, the thought of having some of my favorite '80s hits all on one CD gave me goose bumps (though I couldn't rule out our cold basement as the real source of those bumps).

I went to my music collection and starting pulling out the CDs I would use—Little River Band, Boston, Hall and Oates, Bruce Hornsby and the Range, Billy Joel, Culture Club (yes, I have a Culture Club CD), Starship, REO Speedwagon, Ambrosia, the Village People (everybody has this disc for one song, right?), Luther Vandross... even the Bee Gees! I was in music heaven. After making a list of my favorite songs, I began recording. The CD writer seemed to work well, and it was rather easy. I quickly got the system down and really didn't have to think about the process. All the songs were recording nicely.

Several hours later I finished my "Younger Days Compilation." Amazingly, the kids were still asleep. I wondered if my wife wasn't joking about the cough medicine. I eagerly took my newly completed CD masterpiece and put it into my stereo system. Sitting back, I listened with utter delight. As the songs played, I asked if there could be anything musically better than "hits from the '80s." I told my wife I was in music nirvana. She checked to make sure I hadn't overdosed on the cough syrup.

But I was rocked from my heavenly state in the middle of Toto's hit "Rosanna" by the repeating "d-d-d-d-d" sound that CDs make when they're dirty or scratched. It lasted no more than a couple of seconds and shouldn't have bothered me, but it did. A perfect '80s CD ruined. I took the CD out of the player and checked for a scratch or dirt. I couldn't find any, but I cleaned the CD just in case and put it back into the player. Listening to "Rosanna" again, I hoped for the best. But there it was again, "d-d-d-d-d," in the exact same spot. Now I was sure that the CD wasn't dirty. Something must have happened during the recording process that

I hadn't noticed. It was a faulty recording. The CD was only playing what was burned onto it. It could do nothing else.

What's on Your Disc?

In some wacky ways our brain is like a CD. Over the course of our life, the things we see, hear, smell, taste, and touch are "burned onto" our brain. In fact, data are being written onto our brain continually. Some of that information is being recorded with our complete awareness; other information is recorded without our knowledge. It doesn't matter how the data get there, and it doesn't even matter if the data are good. Our brain uses that information to develop the lenses through which we interpret the world and the people in it. What we have in our brain influences the way we see people, the way we interpret other incoming information, the way we make decisions, and so on. If we have bad data or incomplete information (as a result of a "skip" or a "scratch" in the recording), our actions based on those data may be erroneous.

Here's where we have to be honest with ourselves in analyzing the information we've received about people who are different from us. For example, think about what you have learned in your everyday world about women. How might that influence your opinion about what roles women should have? Critically analyze the information you absorb through the media, whether from television, magazines, billboards, newspapers, or other sources. How are people of color depicted? How might the thousands of images your brain has recorded affect the way you see, treat, and react to people of color? If you go to church, mosque, or synagogue, critically ask yourself how your place of worship thinks about and treats people whose sexual orientation differs from that of the majority. How might that affect the way you think about and treat gay, lesbian, bisexual, and transgendered persons? Think about how you grew up. Did you have a lot of experiences that put you in contact with diverse peoples? Or did you have very few interactions with "different" people? If you did not have many experiences that put you face-to-face with people diversity, assess how that might affect your current thinking about diversity issues.

Data from all these sources influence your thinking at some level, whether you want to admit it or not. Your diversity experiences, or lack thereof, burn information onto your brain. Your reactions to others and their behaviors are a direct result of all the data you've picked up over the years. Like the CD that can play only what was written onto it, whether good or bad, you can act only according to what's in your brain. You can't expect to be unbiased or nondiscriminatory toward others if the information you have about them is biased and discriminatory. Makes sense, doesn't it?

I'm sure you have heard people say things like, "I don't have a biased bone in my body" and "I'm color-blind—I treat everyone the same." Maybe you have uttered such things yourself. Have you ever considered how accurate (or inaccurate) such statements are, in light of how human beings actually gather and use information? If you can come to a better understanding of the information you have about others and the authenticity of that information, you will have taken many steps forward toward living and excelling in an increasingly diverse world. Remember, much like a CD, you tend to play back only what you've recorded.

It's important to understand that you'll never really be able to erase the bad information in your head. It's burned in there permanently, as on a CD. But you can train yourself to be more mindful of how that bad information affects your daily actions, reactions, and decision making. You can learn how to manage the bad information. You also can become more aware of your gut reactions to people who are different from you, and you can question those reactions knowing that they likely are based on stereotypes and biased images. Indeed, a major focus of diversity training is helping people understand and manage their biases because we know we can't completely erase our prejudices. They always will be there, and if we aren't aware of them, they may rear their ugly heads at the worst times. It's not necessarily about intentionality.

Back to my CD and that calm day. My wife suggested I rerecord the song. I reminded her that the system I have does not allow me to rewrite CDs, so she then suggested that I make a new disc. I could have done that, but I'm one of those people who likes to do it right the first time. And it would have meant wasting 70 minutes of other great songs on the CD. Besides, the kids were awakening from their slumber, and my wife had taken away the cough medicine. I would have to listen to the CD as it was, to help remind me that "recording errors" are a fact of life.

Examining the Data

To help you in your efforts to listen to your recordings, here are some questions to ask, an activity, and an assignment for this week.

1. **First glance.** How good is your data about people? What are some examples of things that have been burned onto your brain that you have already realized are faulty data?

2. **Looking inward.** Are you ready to listen to the skips in your recordings? Are you willing to allow them to remind you of your own embedded mistakes? Find one particular skip and try to address it instead of going mindlessly on as the song finishes playing.

3. **What if?** What if some of our recordings are full of skips and scratches about people, values, and differences? How might we separate the good recordings from the bad?

4. **Activity.** In a group, list the attributes of an "ideal twenty-first-century leader"—traits that you and others might want that would motivate and inspire you to peak performance. Now list some attributes you have observed in those given the title "leader" that have been burned onto your own cognitive CD about leadership. How do those two lists compare? What's different? What's the same? How might twenty-first-century leaders differ from twentieth-century leaders, if at all?

5. **This week's assignment.** Critically examine the data sources you implicitly accept as credible. Why are they credible? Could they be wrong or misguided? Find some alternative sources of information that might help you better navigate a twenty-first-century global society.

LEADING AND DOING

"It's no good to have an open-door policy when what's behind the door is a closed mind."
—**Steve L. Robbins**

| 24 |

File Cabinets

Let it be known that I freely and willingly, being under no physical, psychological, or spiritual duress, do hereby declare publicly my love for minivans. Yes, I understand this effectively voids my membership in the Men's Club, but there are times when one must humbly admit, "I had it all wrong."

Like many of my sex, I am genetically predisposed to scorn minivans. However, in the past few years I have discovered a previously hidden but unmistakable affection for a vehicle that my DNA does not hold in high regard. This was not a sudden revelatory flash. It was more like the gradual recognition that having kids is punishment for once having been a kid.

When minivans first arrived on the market, I wondered, "Who could have designed such an eyesore?" Suffice it to say, I once had many negative perceptions of and attitudes toward minivans—and who could blame me? I remember reading a report that affirmed my negativity. As I recall, the research basically said that when a man and a woman are in the front seats of a four-door sedan, 80 percent of the time the man is driving. But when it comes to minivans, the percentages switch: the woman drives 80 percent of the time! It had been ingrained in me that minivans were for the female of the species *Homo sapiens*.

I had only one folder in the mental filing cabinet where I stored information about minivans. All data were thrown into that one folder. When I saw anything that resembled a minivan, that information went into the folder. Chrysler minivans, Ford minivans, Honda minivans—they all looked the same to me. I never got inside any of the vehicles, so I never saw their unique features and personalities. If I had taken a closer look, I might have created subfolders for the different makes and models. But I didn't because, to me, a minivan of any kind was something for women.

And then it happened, an experience so powerful that it began to change my thinking about the world (mostly the part about minivans). My wife and I had a kid…then two, and three, and before I knew it we had four. As all parents know, adding children to your life brings with it tons of stuff: a Pack-n-Play, car seats, toys, diaper bags, clothes, and so on. And when you go on an overnight trip, that stuff comes along. Lugging around baby stuff in a four-door sedan wasn't too bad with one child, and we still managed with two kids. But when child number three was on the way, I came to the dreadful realization that a minivan would park in our garage and that my friends would see me in it—or, worse, they would see me *driving* it.

I brainstormed alternatives. Leaving a couple of kids behind to fend for themselves when we go on trips might work, I thought, but then those pesky people from Child Protective Services would enter the picture. Following my wife in our sedan while she drove the minivan seemed wasteful and expensive. Disguising myself looked like more work than it was worth. In the end, all my calculations produced the same answer: A minivan was in my future.

My future foreseen, I began to take notice of minivans when I saw them on the street. I paid attention to minivan ads in magazines and on TV. I sought out research reporting all the wonderful benefits of minivans. Soon, I could differentiate one minivan from another. I could tell you which ones got a five-star rating on a crash test and which ones didn't. How much horsepower does a Ford Windstar have? I knew that. I knew which models were "sporty" and which ones were "luxury," although the phrase *luxury minivan* struck me as an oxymoron, much like *gourmet takeout.*

I knew there was no turning back when I test-drove my first minivan. I was expecting a clunky, school bus–like ride, but what I experienced felt better than the ride in most of the sedans I'd driven. I test-drove many minivans, even the ones I knew I wouldn't buy, just for the fun of it. Once I got behind the wheel of some minivans, I began to like them. At first, I admired their great utility. Later, I could see how the words *luxury* and *minivan* found each other. Children aside, I was sold on minivans. So today my cognitive minivan folder contains many subfolders. I have a Toyota subfolder, a Honda subfolder, a Ford subfolder, a Chrysler subfolder, a Nissan subfolder, and so on. I recognize their differences. No longer do they all look alike.

I just learned there's a new minivan coming out that has a 260-horsepower V6 motor, twenty-one cup holders, and a 60/40-split rear seat with passenger windows that "roll" down. How cool is that? They're also talking about making an all-wheel-drive version. Now, that's one a twenty-first-century man like me can love…I mean, *use.*

What's in Your Folders?

How many cognitive folders do you have when it comes to people, especially people who are different from you? Do you have just one or many?

Do you have subfolders labeled "Mexican," "Chicano," and "Puerto Rican"? Or do you lump everyone you perceive as Hispanic/Latino into one main folder and think about them all the same way? Do an evaluation of your cognitive folders. Do some of your main folders have more subfolders than others? Is there a diversity of folders that helps you interpret and explain situations and interactions from multiple perspectives? Or do your folders narrow your view of people?

If you have myriad subfolders, is the information correct and complete? It's a good idea to ask yourself where you acquired the information in your folders and how balanced the data are. Did it come from indirect sources (for example, television) that might also have incomplete or incorrect folders, or did it come from real, direct, and balanced interaction with different people? It is said that you can only know what you know. Likewise, your people folders and subfolders are limited to the experiences you've had. In an ever-changing world, it's good to have lots of folders and subfolders about people. The more good information you have, the greater the chance you'll make good decisions when interacting with others. The more knowledge you have about a person, the more you are able to treat him or her as an individual. Conversely, if you have only stereotypical information about someone, you are more likely to treat that person as a stereotype. You are limited in your interactions with people by the information you have in your head about them.

It took a while for me to get my minivan folders and subfolders in shape. In fact, they are still evolving. Each year, I look forward to the introduction of new minivan models so I can enhance my neural network of minivan folders. Do you look forward to meeting and interacting with new, different people so you can increase your network of people folders? If you do, that's great. Do you put yourself in positions that enable you to create new subfolders? If you do, that's awesome! A curiosity about people and the world, coupled with open-mindedness toward entertaining new perspectives, is a powerful combination in an increasingly diverse and complex world. Do you have this combination? Are you intentionally working to get it or to make it stronger? And are you modeling it to others, especially to kids?

Creating New Cognitive Folders

To help you do a check-up on your cognitive folders on a regular basis, here are some questions to ask, an activity, and an assignment for this week.

1. **First glance.** What are some typical "folders" we might have about people and places? Do we label them in a way that keeps us from ever opening them?

2. **Looking inward.** What folders are in your mental file cabinets? Are you able to expand them and make subfolders? Are you eager to enhance your knowledge? How can you enhance your knowledge of others and of the world around you?

3. **What if?** What if your folders are incomplete? What if they have been improperly labeled? Are you courageous enough to add new data, to explore each folder's features?

4. **Activity.** In a group, discuss some of your organization's employee "folders." Do you or your organization tend to toss certain employee types into premade folders? Are some folders open to only a limited set of employees who are of a certain age, gender, culture, or sexual orientation? Talk about how to move employees into a different folder.

5. **This week's assignment.** Add at least one new folder to your cognitive file cabinet or "reclassify" the information in at least one existing folder. You can do this by asking yourself when you might have said, "They're all alike," and then analyzing why you said that.

| 25 |

Wanted: Good Role Models

I dread it when my wife cooks. It's not because she's a bad cook. Far from it. I don't like it when my wife cooks because, in addition to the tasty dishes she makes, she has this thing about health and nutrition that compels her to prepare vegetables. The very existence of vegetables, especially green ones, proves there is a God with a twisted sense of humor. How else do you explain that a class of foods required for a healthy body also makes taste buds curl up and die on contact? As you can see, I am not a big vegetable lover. (And I don't like little vegetables, either.) I tried to find some fondness for veggies and even developed a working relationship with potatoes, corn, and cucumbers. But then I found out that the three I enjoyed are not technically vegetables.

Where did I acquire my disdain for vegetables? My guess is that it resulted from a lack of positive history with vegetables. I did not eat many of them growing up, or if I did I have suppressed most of those traumatic episodes. I do have a rather upsetting recollection of my mother forcing me to eat some spinach when I was 7 years old. I tried to resist by holding the spinach in my mouth for a few hours without swallowing. That, it turns out, is a bad gastronomic strategy. Also, a war of wills is not a good idea when your opponent is a woman whose cultural heritage has endowed her with unflinching patience.

It had been a while since I had felt compelled to eat vegetables, but parental responsibilities have a way of making me do things I'd rather not do. For example, on occasion I like to let out a loud burp, which is a very acceptable thing to do if you're French. It's the French way of showing satisfaction with a meal, and I have a connection with the French. (I took French in high school.)

But belching aloud is not culturally acceptable in the United States, so with kids around I can't just go around burping any time I wish. Let me qualify that: I could, but there are certain consequences. Kids like to do things they see their parents doing. So, if I constantly burp with pride in front of my kids, I shouldn't be surprised to see them doing the same thing, at home or in public. To help my kids grow up in a healthy, culturally acceptable manner, I have to be careful about what I model to them. And this is where we come back to the vegetables. Here is a classic example of how a great dinner can be ruined by the need to display parental leadership.

The family is sitting around the table eagerly awaiting some tasty lasagna. My wife makes great lasagna. Of course, the star ingredient in lasagna is the meat, not the noodles or the tomato sauce or whatever else might not be full of fat and cholesterol. (Cheese, since it has been linked to obesity and clogged arteries, also is an important ingredient. Any true carnivore knows the attributes of real food.) As I fill my plate with the meaty components of the lasagna, I observe my wife placing a steaming dish of green beans on the table, right in front of me. What have I done to deserve this? I run the good-husband checklist through my head: I took out the trash this week, I said, "I love you" numerous times, and it has been a while since I walked into a small room with her, closed the door, and farted. Where did I go wrong?

Trying to ignore the green beans, I dig into my lasagna. I slowly look up to see green beans on all my kids' plates. Then son number three, Jacob, says to me, "Hey, Dad, aren't you going to have some green beans?" (I knew we should have stopped at two kids.)

"I'm not that hungry tonight, Jacob. What I have on my plate is all I need."

Zachary, the second oldest, chimes in, "You should have some, Dad. Mom says they'll make you big and strong." (An only child would have been nice.)

The leader of this pack, Nicholas, senses my vulnerability and swoops in for the kill. "Yeah, Dad, if we have to have them, you have to have them, too."

Now I have no choice. Nicholas has played the "be a good role model" card. Fighting my dread, I scoop a few beans onto my plate. "That's only three," Jacob jumps in. "Have more, Dad. They're good for you." I put some more beans on my plate and keep eating my lasagna. I secretly wish we had a dog that I might discreetly feed the beans to, but accepting the fact that I have to be an omnivore in this family, I eventually clear my plate. I guess this is what it means to be a good parent, a good role model.

I may not like to eat vegetables or to refrain from burping in front of my kids, but I know that it's in their best interest—and mine, too—for me to model those behaviors. If I don't actively teach them the "right stuff," then I will have to accept some responsibility for any unwanted behavior they display in the future.

Over the course of time I have grown to like some of the vegetables my wife and kids have "forced" me to eat. I'm just hoping that no one bursts my bubble one day by informing me that carrots and spinach are not vegetables.

Are You Eating Your Veggies?

How good are you and the other leaders in your organization about "eating your veggies"—that is, modeling inclusive, culturally competent behavior to others, whether they are supervisors, colleagues, your staff, kids, or friends? Are you mindful of what you are teaching to and reinforcing in others through your actions? What do you and the other leaders do when you hear a demeaning joke? What action do you take when you recognize that nonmajority voices are not being heard? To encourage people in your organization to attend cultural competence training, are you willing to go first? What about your CEO?

If you want your employees to respect and engage different perspectives, do you let them see you doing those things? Telling is not as powerful as showing that it's good to have relationships with people who see the world differently from the way you do. Behavioral messages are much more compelling than verbal messages, and when the two conflict, the walk overpowers the talk. I get a kick out of parents who, after learning that their kids have shown disrespect to someone who is "different," say something like, "We don't teach our kids prejudice," or, "My kids don't learn that at home." Sometimes the question is not what we are actively teaching but what people are subtly learning from our actions or our lack of action.

If you want your employees, kids, or others to look to you for leadership in inclusion and diversity, are you truly willing to engage in the same process of learning and experiencing that you want for them? Do you have close friends who are different from you? Are you willing to feel initial discomfort to explore realities different from your own? Can you entertain new ideas, new perspectives, and new ways of doing things with an open mind and a positive attitude? These are some of the attributes of a culturally competent person, attributes that are becoming increasingly more important in a twenty-first-century world in which our encounters with difference and that which is new will only increase.

Walking on the Role Model Runway

In all that we do, we model behavior in some way, to someone. To help you assess your modeling ability, here are some questions to ask, an activity, and an assignment for this week.

1. **First glance.** What is being modeled in your organization? Are you and other leaders practicing what you preach? How might your actions reinforce or contradict your organization's values and mission?

2. **Looking inward.** What are you modeling to the people around you? Are you engaged in the process of learning and appreciating new "vegetables"? If not, what veggies are on your "yuck" list?

3. **What if?** What if you might really enjoy the vegetables you have yet to taste? How will you know unless you try them? What if some vegetables enhance the flavor of the rest of the meal?

4. **Activity.** In a group, discuss how your organization respects and engages different or new perspectives. Determine some areas of success and others that need improvement. What are some of the vegetables your organization shies away from? How might your leaders better model different behaviors and attitudes necessary in an increasingly diverse society?

5. **This week's assignment.** Try something new and different. Eat at a different restaurant. Read a different book. See a different movie. Make a new friend.

| 26 |
Swimming's Great, Just Don't Get Me Wet

My son Zachary has been taking swimming lessons on and off for the past year. Now, as a 4-year-old (oops, 4-and-a-half-year-old—he reminds me often of this important distinction), he is starting to prove that little people do not necessarily sink in a watery environment. Don't get me wrong, no one observing him would compare him to an Olympic swimmer, but the signs of progress are there.

But this story is not about Zachary. It's about the swimming teacher who was running a class at the other end of the pool one day when I was present for Zachary's lesson. The teacher stood at the edge of the pool with a towel wrapped around her waist and took attendance. Her students looked a little older than Zachary, probably 5 or 6 years old. It was obvious that they had not yet mastered the art of swimming, either, but they were a little further along on their journey than my son.

As I watched Zachary in his lesson, I glanced over at this other class to see if it would be appropriate for my son's next stage of training. What surprised me as I watched wasn't that the kids flailed in the water like hooked fish, but that the teacher had not joined them in the pool. She continued to stand on the side, barking out instructions, "Long arms, reach and pull, 1, 2, 3, 4, breathe, reach and pull." The instruction sounded good, like she knew what she was talking about. Surely, she soon would jump into the pool to offer more detailed instruction and to model the correct techniques.

As I continued to watch, part of me wanted to go over and push the teacher in. Fifteen minutes into the lesson, she remained dry. Now, instead of being perplexed, I was starting to be impressed by this new method. "What a novel idea," I thought, teaching swimming from afar without getting wet. When one of her students needed some assistance, the teacher walked over, knelt down, and made some motions showing what she wanted the student to do. That towel remained around her waist; she was still dry. Clearly, the teacher had no intention of entering the pool on this particular day, and I began to wonder: Was there something wrong with her today? Did her doctor tell her not to get wet? Does she know how to swim?

I suppose swimming can be taught without getting wet, but I never saw that method when I learned how to swim, nor did those teaching my son take that approach. I couldn't make sense of it. It might make a little sense if the students were more accomplished swimmers and did not require so much instruction, but this definitely was not the case.

Teaching swimming to beginners without getting in the water, without getting in the environment, seems counterintuitive to me. While it may work to some degree, it does not seem like the most effective method of instruction. It doesn't seem like it would produce the best outcome.

Are You in the Water?

With this swimming teacher in mind, I pose these questions to everyone responsible for diversity initiatives in her or his organization: Is this how some key people in your organization, especially leaders, approach diversity? Can you see signs that your organization wants to swim, but doesn't want to dive in?

Often, when the "swim but don't get wet" approach is taken, inclusion and diversity initiatives are seen as extracurricular rather than integral to the daily operations and growth of a company. This produces a "to-do list" mentality, where actions tend to be seen as separate, unconnected events, definitely not strategic. Moreover, when times get tough economically, diversity initiatives are among the first in line at the chopping block. So take a critical look at your diversity initiatives to see if they might need a push into the pool. A "let's get wet" commitment is crucial to the success of any diversity initiative. And when I say wet, I mean fully immersed, not just feet-in-the-water. Anything less allows us to feel good and to stay comfortable but does little to produce desired outcomes.

Are you ready to jump in? The initial entry may not feel that great. But stay a while and you'll likely find the waters of diversity to be quite refreshing.

Time to Get All Wet

Are you ready to take the towel off and jump into the water? To facilitate your entry, here are some questions to ask, an activity, and an assignment for this week.

1. **First glance.** How does this story relate to your organization? Are your leaders fully immersed in inclusion and diversity or standing at the edge of the pool? What is the former? What is the latter? Can you recognize the difference?

2. **Looking inward.** How might you jump in? What are some ways that you might progress beyond getting your feet wet and totally immerse yourself? Are inclusion and diversity an integral part of your daily life?

3. **What if?** What if some swimmers have more experience in the pool? What if your own teachers never got wet? How might you learn from their experiences?

4. **Activity.** Discuss your organization's strategic vision for inclusion and diversity. What types of swimming lessons are needed to reach your goals? Are your teachers in the pool or standing on the edge? Take some time to write out how you might make "getting wet" a routine part of your workday, your professional development, and your corporate culture.

5. **This week's assignment.** Find a way to immerse yourself in the waters of inclusion and diversity. You might even get others wet! For example, begin learning a new language—not by using a DVD or a book, but by engaging with people who speak the language you want to learn.

| 27 |

Use One More Club

It's late February and there's a half-foot of snow on the ground, but I am thinking golf. Why not? The pro golf tour started weeks ago, teasing me every weekend as if to say, "Hey, you, sitting in your winter wonderland, watch us play golf in lush Hawaii, warm Florida, and sunny California. And by the way, we're making truckloads of money hitting a little white ball, and you're not."

If you're a golfer stuck in a wintry state like Michigan, you have the bug by February. And if you have the bug, you are a "real" golfer. (Note that I didn't say "good" golfer. Being a real golfer and being a good golfer can be mutually exclusive things.) We real golfers are an odd bunch, itching to spend hundreds, even thousands of dollars every golf season in an effort to improve our game by one or two strokes. Our hard-earned money gets sucked into a big black hole so that we can tell others how well we sank a little ball into a little black hole. We dream of telling people we knocked a 200-yard 4-iron stiff, within two feet of the flag, and we tend to leave out the part about three-putting the remaining two-footer.

For me and, I suspect, for many other golfers, every season begins the same way. We have glorious visions of consistently driving 250-plus yards…and straight. We see ourselves using 8-irons to send the ball flying 165 yards, though our history suggests otherwise. Our thoughts are filled with mentally-draining 15-foot putts, memories of missed two-footers purged by the cleansing snow—or maybe by playing with people who offer generous "gimmes."

This year, for my "become a better golfer" project, I have written the words "take one more club." When practicing, I can hit with my 8-iron as far as 160 yards (okay, 150 yards). For some reason, I believe I can hit that distance with my 8-iron when I play on the course. Like me, many golfers are overly optimistic. They believe if they can do something in practice three times out of 10, then they certainly should be able to do it on the course nine times out of 10. And they get angry when it doesn't happen that way. They have a really good attitude about great execution, but that positive attitude rarely translates to the desired outcome.

The golfer's mentality is much like the duality suggested by Greek philosopher Socrates, who postulated that there exist primarily two worlds—the perfect and the imperfect. In the perfect world, I routinely hit my 8-iron 160 yards (okay, 150). Able to execute perfectly every time, I don't have to worry about sand traps, the long grass in back of the green, or the water in front. These obstacles do not come into play in my perfect world because my shots are perfect.

In my imperfect world, however, those obstacles are real. In that world, misplaced divots are my trademarks. Big ones, little ones, thick ones, and thin ones—it's not unusual for chunks of earth and grass to fly farther than my ball. I am targeted by golf course maintenance crews for extinction in my imperfect world, where 8-iron shots erratically fly only 140 yards. I would be much better off if I took one more club.

What Course Are You Playing On?

The duality of perfect and imperfect worlds extends beyond golf. We think we do things and behave exceedingly well in other areas of life, too. "Of course I'm not biased. No way do I have prejudice. I treat everyone the same. I judge only on ability." These are words found in the perfect world. And somehow they've made their way to the imperfect world, the real world.

When it comes to inclusion and diversity, we all have a tendency to think of ourselves as relatively perfect. Sure, we make mistakes, but they are few. Seeing ourselves in an overly positive, optimistic light can blind us to the imperfections in our daily interactions. In our perfect world, many of us embrace and value the concept of diversity. So we find it difficult to accept the notion that we don't "do diversity" well. Realistically, we should not be surprised when we make mistakes because many of us rarely practice diversity in our everyday interactions. In that way, diversity is much like golf.

We golfers expect to play well even if we don't practice (which for most golfers means slapping balls on the range for five minutes before tee time—isn't that enough?). We then wonder why, in the heat of competition with 25 cents on the line, we buckle under the pressure of a two-foot putt.

How many of us give ourselves the opportunity to practice interacting with others who are different from us? Or do we just expect to execute correctly when the time arises? Face it, unless we prepare and practice for the changing realities of our world, we shouldn't be shocked when our attempts at "doing diversity" fall short. Just as it is hard to hit a golf ball well if we don't practice consistently and regularly, it's difficult to be good at inclusion and diversity when we don't engage diversity consistently and practice inclusion regularly.

Living out inclusion and diversity, like life, is a journey of error correction. And if that is true, the question for all of us becomes, "Are we willing to admit our mistakes and courageous enough to correct them?"

Practicing Your Swing

How good is your inclusion and diversity swing? To help you practice getting better, here are some questions to ask, an activity, and an assignment for this week.

1. **First glance.** Where do your optimistic realities cloud the realities of your imperfect world? What dualities of the perfect and imperfect worlds exist in your organization?

2. **Looking inward.** How often do you practice relating to differences in ethnicity, religion, or orientation? When do you find yourself buckling under the pressure of seemingly "easy" shots?

3. **What if?** What if we don't all play with the same golf clubs? What if some people get more practice time than others? What if practicing inclusion and diversity doesn't take as much time as you thought it would? What if you don't practice? What if your inclusion and diversity bag is one (or several) clubs short of a full set? What if you don't have a bag? Or clubs?

4. **Activity.** Have the group write down the qualities, characteristics, and actions that would fall under the category of "doing inclusion and diversity well" in your organization. Describe the "perfect world" of inclusion. Now take an honest look at the real world—your imperfect world that you engage in and work in every day. On the opposite side of your "perfect world" list, note some real opportunities for growth and improvement in reaching your "optimistic vision." Write up a practice plan for yourself and for groups in your organization.

Practicing Your Swing (cont'd)

5. **This week's assignment.** Get out a new club and practice a new swing. As an idea, make it a point to have lunch with people with whom you rarely or never have lunch. If not lunch, take advantage of a coffee break.

| 28 |

Nubby Sandals

We recently welcomed a newborn into our family—Natalie, our fourth child. Bringing her home brought back a lot of great memories of our other children as infants. However, it also ushered out something we hold dear: sleep!

As newborn babies go, Natalie has been pretty easy. But she does have moments (or hours) when she likes to punish her mom and dad for putting her through nine months of cramped living. One of those moments occurred when Natalie was just a few weeks old.

My wife had just fed Natalie around 11:00 p.m. and it was bedtime. At least it was our bedtime. But Natalie had other plans, and she started to cry. So, being the thoughtful dad and husband that I am, I took my turn with Natalie.

When our other kids had cried as newborns, I had taken them for a nice car ride or a walk. This time I thought I'd combine the two and take a trip to our local open-all-night grocery store. As I got ready to head out the door, I was unable to find my sandals, so I squeezed into my wife's.

They looked like ordinary sandals, but they felt uniquely good. They had a bunch of little nubs on the insole that are designed to stimulate the bottoms of your feet. And they did a good job of it.

So, with a couple of stimulated feet, I went off with Natalie to take our midnight ride and walk. As I pushed Natalie around the store I thought about how nice my feet felt wearing my wife's sandals. Whoever had thought of putting those nubs on the insoles was a genius. I thought about writing a letter to the manufacturers to tell them how good the sandals felt. But that was a fleeting thought.

Ten minutes in the store turned into 20 and I became aware of the sandals again. Those little nubs were starting to hurt. The more I walked, the more they hurt. After 50 minutes of walking around the store, my feet were killing me. Fortunately, by that time Natalie had fallen asleep, so I could go home and take off those nubby sandals.

The next day, I told my wife about my trip to the store with Natalie and asked her how she could walk in those things. "They hurt me at first, too," she replied matter-of-factly, "but I kept wearing them, and pretty soon not only didn't they hurt, they actually felt good." I told her I'd stick with my nubless sandals.

Do Your Sandals Hurt?

Upon reflection, I began to see a connection between my experiences with my wife's sandals and the way many people and organizations initially experience diversity. Many well-meaning people become passionate about diversity and want to do something right away. Individuals participate in a workshop or attend an inspiring conference. Organizations start observing "diversity week" or examine their workforce for minority participation. Just as those nubby sandals initially made my feet feel good, these people and organizations naturally feel good about what they are doing. But then the honeymoon feeling wears off, the nubs start to hurt, and the real work begins.

Being intentional about experiencing and understanding different people and cultures is difficult. For example, creating a diverse supplier base to ensure opportunities for veterans, people of color, women, and others who have been historically left out is not easy. Objecting when a coworker makes an "I didn't mean anything by it" racist joke is tough. Confronting a person who regularly engages in subtle slights to devalue people (e.g., a nonverbal gesture that communicates dislike of or disgust for another's idea) is uncomfortable. These actions are like those nubby sandals: They hurt. Are you and your organization willing to persevere through the pain? Are you prepared to be diligent after the easy stuff passes? Are you willing to walk not just one mile but many in another's shoes? Sometimes the first mile is the easy one. It's the journey that follows that too many people and organizations are unwilling to embark on. But if you are committed, the rewards can be many.

So take a walk in those nubby inclusion and diversity sandals. There will likely be pain involved, but if you stick it out, you will reap the rewards that inclusion and diversity offer.

Learning to Walk the Walk

To help you facilitate discussion around the long-term benefits of persevering through the "nubs" along the way to inclusion and diversity, here are some questions to ask, an activity, and an assignment for this week.

1. **First glance.** How is your diversity journey going? Are you just beginning, or have you already run into some painful nubs? What about your organization—any nubs yet?

2. **Looking inward.** What are some experiences in your life in which endurance paid off in the end? What did you learn from those experiences that you might never have learned otherwise?

3. **What if?** What if your corporate sandals are nubless? Does that mean you've solved all the diversity issues? Or have you stopped trying or not gone deeply enough?

4. **Activity.** Have the group examine your organization's diversity goals. What are some goals your company has set that have lost their new-toy luster? List reasons why the honeymoon feeling might have faded. What actions are necessary to continue the journey toward those goals? What obstacles will you need to overcome? What rewards will you reap on the other side?

5. **This week's assignment.** Feel the nubs. Stand up and object to that racist joke your coworker told.

CHANGING
THE
ORGANIZATION

"Diversity is about your mix of people. Inclusion is
about how well your people mix."
—**Steve L. Robbins**

| 29 |
Membership Has Its Privileges

Do you recall this tagline "Membership Has Its Privileges"? Of course you do! This memorable advertising campaign by American Express from way, way back in the twentieth century was developed to let you know you were special...*if* you had an American Express credit card. Holders of such cards were given benefits others did not receive. And the benefits were many.

Amex cardholders had exclusive, early access to tickets for special sporting events and music concerts. Even today, my wife and I, as cardholders, have the privilege of purchasing tickets to the United States Open Tennis Championships held in New York before the general public gets the chance. Sometime around May of every year, we receive an email telling us about our special privilege. Looking to vacation in an exotic place and hang out with exotic people? It can be yours with an Amex card. Want to have your own dedicated concierge phone line for personal shopping, or to tell you what concierge means? Yep, it's all yours with an Amex card.

Indeed, membership has its privileges. You get those privileges and more as part of joining the American Express tribe. All you have to do is sign up and give your John Henry; Social Security number; banking information; and, of course, your email address so the nice folks at American Express can inform you of even more exclusive cards that can provide even more exclusive privileges.

Unlike American Express, some groups allow membership without signing up or having to do any work for entry. You may think these types of groups can't offer highly valued privileges, as they are open to all, but you would be wrong. Take this group of which I am a member. By the way, it's highly likely you are in this tribe as well and aren't even aware of it. Amazingly, the vast majority of the human population finds itself as members of this group. It's a not-so-secret secret underground group known as, wait for it... Right-Handers!

Unaware and unrecognized, most of us hold membership in the Right-Hander tribe. Various estimates peg us Right-Handers as comprising approximately 90 percent of the population. So, while we're not exactly exclusive, we do have exclusive benefits—benefits that the other 10 percent, the Lefties, do not receive. Because we live in a world built for right-handers, you might say we have Right-Hander privilege.

What are some of these privileges exclusively bestowed upon Right-Handers? Well, to get a better understanding, I took it upon myself to do some basic qualitative research with those Lefties. Here's what I uncovered. Oh, just to warn the other Right-Handers out there, this will blow your mind. One of the first things the Lefties mentioned is that they like being Lefties, but it can be inconvenient at times. When I asked about those inconveniences, they rattled off a list of items and instances they found bothersome. Number one on that list? Scissors and other assorted hand tools. While the list is growing, relatively few tools are designed with Lefties in mind. A close second on the list of irritations is right-handed desks. Quite a few others mentioned spiral-bound note-books and a writing system that forces one to write from left to right, especially with an overly "inky" ink pen. However, this complaint was not shared by the younger Lefties I talked to, since they weren't quite sure how to use a pen. One Lefty enlightened me to the fact that Righties get to leave their watch on when they change the time, because the little thingamajig used to adjust the time is on the right-hand side of the watch. Most Lefties must take their watch off. Oh, did you know that good steak knives are serrated in one direction? They cut better for the Righty. I did not know that. In fact, it never crossed my mind. I have the privilege of not having to be bothered by this culinary asymmetry.

Some said it was hard to find a guitar built for Lefties. It's not that they aren't out there; it just takes longer to find good ones. If you like shooting rifles, you better make sure the bullet casing doesn't smack you in the face after firing your round. A few mentioned some difficulty with driving a car with a manual transmission and thus a stick shift. They didn't take kindly when I suggested they go live in England. Suffice it to say, the Lefties I spoke with were very aware that they live in a world not built for them. It hits them on a regular, if not daily, basis that they're "outsiders" in a world constructed for Right-Handers. While it's evident for Lefties, I doubt that awareness holds true for us Righties.

So, let me pose a few questions to all of us Right-Handers, and be honest in answering. How often, if ever, do we take notice that the world we live in has been built for us? How many of us are even aware that we live in an asymmetric world when it comes to "directional handed-ness"? Have we Righties ever pondered what it might be like to have to navigate a world built for Lefties? My guess is that most of us Righties spend little, if any, precious cognitive energy considering the relative ease and com-fort of living in a world built for us. We just kind of assume the benefits and privileges we have as Righties are bestowed upon everyone. Or maybe more accurately, we don't even think of having any advantage as a Righty. And if we have any so-called privileges, they were all earned through hard work and sound decision making.

But here's the deal. When we Righties don't recognize that we live in a world designed to make our lives easier, it's highly likely we don't recognize that that same world makes the lives of others, well, shall we say, less easy. At times, Lefties in a Right-Hander's world spend a little more time and energy doing the same things Righties do. It often takes extra time and energy going from store to store to find left-handed golf clubs or a left-handed baseball glove. I'm sure it would take me, a Right-Hander, more time to open a can if I had to use a can opener made for Lefties. And I'd eat up a lot of cognitive energy being frustrated during the process. I imagine it's a bit tiring at times to be a Left-Hander in a Right-Hander's world.

And here's the kicker: When I, the Righty, the insider, don't recognize the different lived experiences between Righties and Lefties, how frustrating or tiring it might be to be the Lefty, the outsider, I might inadvertently pour salt into the proverbial wound. I've done this multiple times when our family goes out to dinner.

My wife and I have four children. One is a Lefty. When we have the occasion to eat out together, as we are being seated, I often say to my Lefty son, "Hey, Zach, sit over here so you don't bump your Righty brothers or sister when you eat." I don't ever recall telling our Right-Handed kids to make seating adjustments for their Left-Handed brother so that he is not inconvenienced.

In a sense, this is what I'm saying to my Left-Handed son: "Hey, Zach, Lefty, Outsider, use some of your already-depleted cognitive resources to make sure the Righties, the insiders, who are already comfortable, well, more comfortable." Because I am unaware or forget that there are, at times, meaningful and substantive differences between

186

Righties and Lefties and how they live their lives, it doesn't occur to me that I am asking my Lefty son to do things I do not ask my Righty kids to do. Unknowingly, I am giving my Right-Handed children preferential treatment as Righties. Yes, membership has its privileges.

My disparate treatment of my kids based on "handedness" is not because I dislike Lefties. It's not that I am not nice. It's because I fail to notice that, when it comes to handedness, we operate in a nonneutral, asymmetric environment where Righties experience benefits and privileges to which Lefties have no access. I have what one might call "Right-Hander Privilege." One of those privileges, interestingly enough, is the privilege not to be reminded that the environments I walk in are generally built for me.

Now take the term "Right-Hander Privilege" and replace "Right-Hander" with other descriptors, like "Male," as in Male Privilege. How about "Wealth," as in Wealth Privilege? In some situations, it's Republican or Democrat Privilege. At times it's Christian Privilege or Heterosexual Privilege. In a hospital it might be Physician Privilege; in a company with multiple locations, it might be Home Office Privilege. In a high-tech organization, it could be Engineer Privilege. And sometimes, because of a nation's history, it's White Privilege. Get the idea?

Having "privilege" is not necessarily a bad thing. All things equal I'd rather have privilege than not. Whether privilege can be considered good or bad, positive or negative, is more a function of what you do with the privilege you have when you recognize that you have it. An important first step is to be more mindful and recognize the times and situations when one might have privilege(s). This can be hard for some because, for various reasons, there are people who don't want to admit there are times when they have advantages and benefits that others do not have. Some can't accept they have or had it a little easier than others under certain circumstances. Still others lack the knowledge and/or experiences to understand that their accomplishments may have been achieved on an uneven playing field, or that they got to play on a field that others did not have opportunity even to warm up on.

At any given time, we have all experienced the privileges of being a member of a special group. As you navigate your world, try to be more mindful of when you might have benefits and privileges that others don't have. Try to understand how the benefits and privileges you have are "earned" or even "unearned." It might also be helpful to take notice of the times you might NOT have certain advantages that others have, especially advantages that derive from just plain-old membership in a group to which you do not have access. I hope you will take some new-found knowledge of privilege and not only educate others who may not have the same awareness you have, but also use any privilege you in the service of others.

Becoming Aware of Benefits

To help you become more aware of the invisible nature of "privileges and benefits," here are some questions to ask, an activity, and an assignment for this week.

1. **First glance.** How does your organization's culture and ways of thinking and doing offer benefits/advantages to some but not to others? Is that positive or negative?

2. **Looking inward.** What are some privileges you've received by being a member of certain groups? Think about whether these privileges are earned or unearned.

3. **What if?** What if you have blind spots with respect to privileges, meaning you don't notice the privileges given to you but not to others? How could you discover what these blind spots are?

4. **Activity.** In a small group, share how you've noticed how people respond when they are confronted with the idea that they have privileges others do not have merely by being a member of a particular group.

5. **This week's assignment.** Identify the privileges you might have and find a way to use these privileges to help others.

| 30 |

It's the System, Stupid

"Dad, there's bees in the house!" my 2-year-old son shouted from downstairs. Figuring my son was referring to the Pooh video he was watching, I leisurely made my way down to our family room, not at all expecting to see any yellow-and-black-striped insects. But when I got downstairs, my son was not watching the video. He was staring intently at the ceiling lights.

"Whatcha looking at, Jacob?" I asked.

"The bees. There's bees up there." I looked up but didn't see anything. Wanting to do what all the "be a good father" books tell me to do, I played along to encourage my child's imagination.

"Wow, Jacob, there are bees, lots of them."

"Not lots, Dad, just two. See," he said, pointing to a specific light. "Just two."

Again I looked but didn't see anything. I continued to play along. "Yep, just two." I walked over to give Jacob a hug. As I reached down toward him, I heard a faint buzzing noise from above. I looked up to see a bee flying around. My son barked out, "Get the kill-bugger! Get the kill-bugger!"

I jumped to my feet. "What's a kill-bugger?"

"You know, a kill-bugger," he replied. "Mommy uses it to dead the bees."

Thoughts raced through my head—kill-bugger, Mommy, bees, golf season's almost over, I have to pee. Then, it clicked: He meant the flyswatter!

I rushed upstairs to get the "kill-bugger" and a long-sleeved shirt and a pair of gloves to protect myself from a bee that was one one-thousandth my size. Then, in full armor and brandishing the fly-swatter, I ran downstairs to find the bee. Within minutes, I located my prey, which had brought friends. With two quick, surgical swats (okay, maybe five or six) I showed those bees why humans are atop the food chain. As a rite of passage, I handed my son the flyswatter and let him take a couple of swipes at the bees lying motionless on the carpet. With the hunt over, my son helped me dispose of the unfortunate creatures.

Returning the flyswatter to its place upstairs, I wondered how the bees had entered the house. Maybe they had just flown in when a door was left open. But Jacob had mentioned that Mommy had "deaded" other bees, so I checked with my wife. She told me she had figured the bees were coming through some vent in the basement, but she hadn't had time to test her theory.

Believing my wife would take care of the bee situation, I didn't give it another thought. But the next day I had to pull out the kill-bugger for another assignment—and again the next day, and the day after that, and the day after that. It was kind of fun at first, but by the fifth day I was becoming perturbed.

This went on for a couple of weeks. The bees kept coming in, one by one, and every day I carved a few more notches on the kill-bugger. It definitely was no longer fun now, especially after my 7-year-old gave me a lecture about how bees are harmless and necessary. So, to spare myself—and the bees—future grief, I decided to look for the bees' entrance.

After several hours of searching I found the breach in security. It was the radon gas tube that runs from our basement to the outside, allowing potentially deadly radon gas to escape. I covered the tube with a mesh screen. Since then I have not had to go on any more bee hunts.

Reflecting on this ordeal, I realized that the bees were just doing what bees do, flying around looking for food and plants to pollinate. The problem was the tube that allowed the bees to enter our house. Unfortunately, I killed about 20 bees before I figured out how to resolve the issue.

A number of innocent, hardworking bees lost their lives unnecessarily. For some reason, I had seen the bees as the problem. Once I figured out that the system (i.e., the structure of the house) needed fixing, I was able to come up with a permanent solution that was better both for the bees and for my family.

Are You Killing Bees?

Organizations sometimes rush to blame performance problems on their people rather than looking at organizational structures, systems, and ways of doing things (the organizational culture) to determine their cause. When we perceive that a problem lies with an individual, we develop solutions targeted at individuals. But what if the problem, or a large part of it, lies with the organization? For example, what if an organizational culture that prides itself on hard work, on 50-60–hour workweeks, goes overboard? Could performance problems often blamed on uncommitted slackers actually be the result of overcommitted doers being afraid to say no because the culture punishes those who do so?

"Fixing" individuals when the problem stems from the system only ensures that there will always be people to fix. If our organizational surveys tell us that certain groups (women, people of color, or older persons, for example) are less likely to get hired or promoted than other groups, then a certain mental bell should ring—one that wakes us up to problems in the system. If some groups of employees have consistently higher turnover rates compared to others, then we should recognize that there might be an underlying problem with the way those groups are being treated—or at least with the way they perceive they are being treated. In general, a high turnover rate in one group suggests that there might be a system problem, not necessarily a people problem.

Poor employee performance can result from a number of things, including cultural factors such as stress, exclusion, and lack of opportunity. But if we rarely consider the influence of organizational culture, then we are likely to see employees as underperforming people rather than as people who could thrive in the right environment.

Some people in our organizations are seen as "problem people," and we deal with them from that perspective. But our approach might change if we were to recognize that their issues could be the result of systemic, or organizational, flaws. This idea, however, is often hard for people in managerial or leadership positions to accept. Their feeling is, "If I can make it, why can't they?" They tend to overlook the disproportionate number of barriers that impede some people and not others.

Does your system or organizational culture include everyone? Or does it subtly say, "If you look and act a certain way, you'll do fine here"? If the latter is true, and you want to be able to attract and retain the best and brightest in a more diverse world, then changes must be made. The first step might be accepting that systems and cultural issues may be at the root of some observable people issues and that fixing people could be a waste of time, energy, and money. The major impetus behind the "fixing people" approach is that it's easier to fix people (that is, get rid of them) than to fix systems. Fixing systems can be a long, slow, and painful process, but if done right it can produce sustainable, lasting benefits for all.

Covering Holes in the System

Begin finding and fixing structural problems instead of trying to fix people. To help you look for "holes" in your system, here are some questions to ask, an activity, and an assignment for this week.

1. **First glance.** Do you see innocent bees taking the blame in your organization? Where are your people problems?

2. **Looking inward.** How do you handle the bees you encounter? Do you think to look for structural issues?

3. **What if?** What if those bees are just symptoms of structural problems? What if you saw what the bees see?

4. **Activity.** Outline some of your organization's people problems. Discuss how these might be symptoms of a systemic problem rather than isolated people issues. How might your organization begin the work of understanding its structural weaknesses? What kinds of feedback (from the bees?) might provide important data?

5. **This week's assignment.** Look at a situation from the perspective of the bees. For example, if you are currently getting around fine, try navigating your workplace or community using a wheelchair or crutches.

| 31 |

A New Search Routine

There is a chorus that rings incessantly through our house: "Where's my Game Boy game?" Once benign background noise, it now evokes a response that generally requires anger management therapy.

I bought this thing called a Game Boy several years ago for my eldest son, Nicholas. At the time I was unaware of the troubles it would bring. What I thought was a cool electronic toy that hip dads buy for their kids has turned into a frequent source of mental and emotional frustration.

Looking back, I can see how my genetic predisposition to acquire high-tech gadgets clouded my ordinarily strong decision-making skills. (I can also see my wife laughing as I write this. Yeah, I know it sounds overly dramatic, but sometimes you have to rationalize bad decisions.)

Anyway, the Game Boy entered our home. There were few problems at first, primarily because Nicholas had only one game cartridge. (When you buy a Game Boy unit you also have to buy game cartridges.) If there is only one game cartridge, it is always in the unit and presumably can't get lost. But when you have more than one cartridge, the ones that aren't plugged into the Game Boy often get misplaced. And that's when that increasingly annoying chorus rings out.

Nicholas quickly learned the words after getting his second Game Boy game cartridge. The refrain was tolerable at first—as a solo. But in another lapse of judgment, I purchased a Game Boy for our second son, Zachary. So now my wife and I hear, "Where's my Game Boy game?" in two-part harmony.

To be fair, it's not really the Game Boys that are the problem; it's the kids who play them. Here is a recent exchange between my sons and me that illustrates this point. It had been a quiet, relaxing evening, allowing my wife and me to spend some time with each other—the 10 minutes of daily quality time typical of US couples. And then it started.

Running up the stairs, Zachary asked, "Where's my Game Boy game?"

"I don't know. Where did you put it?" I answered. "Which one are you looking for?"

"I can't find Pokémon Silver Version. I looked everywhere." Frustration flooded through his words.

"And I can't find Pokémon Ruby Version," Nicholas chimed in.

"I suppose you looked everywhere, too?"

"Yep, Zachary and I looked in all the places we've played our Game Boys. We looked in our room, the toy room, and the car," Nicholas said.

"How about Jacob's room, or Natalie's room, or the back room?" I asked with growing impatience.

Confidently, Zachary replied, "Our games aren't in those places. We never play them there."

I commended Zachary on his use of logic but told him that I had seen his little sister, Natalie, playing in her room with something that looked very much like a Game Boy game cartridge. "Let's go look there," I said.

As we walked in, the boys made a quick scan of the room. "See, I told ya, Dad!" Zachary said. "They aren't in here." Nicholas said nothing, continuing to look.

"Look harder, Zach, like your brother's doing."

Reluctantly, Zachary made a more thorough investigation. He and Nicholas looked under Natalie's chairs, behind her dresser, by her crib... no cartridges.

"Check in the corner, behind the crib," I suggested.

Nicholas took a peek. "Here they are!" he exclaimed. "And there's more than the Pokémon games. Here's the F-14 Fighter game you've been looking for, Zach."

I looked at Zachary, trying to suppress an "I told you so" but failing. Zachary smiled innocently and said, "It's not our fault we couldn't find the games at first. They've never been in Natalie's room. We've never had to look there before. They've always been downstairs."

With a stash of Game Boy game cartridges in hand, Nicholas and Zachary rushed out of Natalie's room. Then, as I was about to leave the room, Zachary came around the corner, gave me a hug, and said, "Thanks, Dad, for showing us another place to look for our games when they get lost." Ahh, all is now right in the world of parenting.

How Hard Are You Looking?

The message here is for those who may have some reservations about affirmative action in terms of hiring and promotion. However you define affirmative action, it has, in concept, always encouraged us to look in places that have been off our radar screen. It's about "forcing" us to do things that we should have been doing in the first place, especially in a country that prides itself on equality, fairness, and justice.

If you and your organization want to find the best people representing diverse experiences and perspectives, then you must search in new places, places you've never even thought of searching. This search requires you to consider more than just the doors that you've always used. Door #1 and door #2 may have produced good, qualified employees in the past and likely will do so in the future. But don't be blind to door #3, #4, #5, and #6. Progressive, enlightened organizations committed to inclusion and diversity (read: maybe your competitors) will be looking behind those doors. And they will find some of the best and brightest in the places you've been overlooking.

If you are committed to and intentional about changing your search routine, you will find that "disabled" people are not as disabled as you might think. Or that Asians are good at much more than just math. You might discover that many women are extraordinary leaders who would outdo many men if given the opportunity. How might your organization be enriched if you opened some new doors and found that many older people keep going with great fervor beyond age sixty-five? Or that a Morehead State graduate can outshine a Harvard alum? And what if people with non-European accents have talents and skills that extend beyond the shop floor?

Doors unopened are opportunities unclaimed. But don't just open the door for a quick scan, as my sons did. Stay a while, make a thorough search, and do it with sincerity. The people you seek may need to get better acquainted with you before they decide it's safe to connect. Reaching out to audiences that harbor suspicion (because you were not there in the past) will require a sustained effort. It's often a matter of trust, and one "help wanted" posting in an ethnic newspaper usually doesn't cut it. This is just one small step in the journey that builds trust in communities that historically have been neglected.

By making sincere, ongoing efforts to look in places you've never looked before, you are taking affirming action. If more people and organizations took affirming action, there would be little need for affirmative action policies. Such policies, still necessary, stem from a history of legal and societal doors being slammed in the face of people who were the "wrong" race, gender, age, religion, and so on.

It will take time, energy, and commitment to change hiring and promotion strategies that are ineffective in the face of increasing diversity. It will require people becoming truly committed to creating a level playing field by first examining and then changing their attitudes, beliefs, and practices. Making that commitment to change—to recognize and open other doors—is the essence of affirming action.

Finding New Places to Look

To help you discuss and find some new doors to look behind and new places to search, here are some questions to ask, an activity, and an assignment for this week.

1. **First glance.** Does your organization habitually look for talent in the same places? How are you recruiting talent that will complement your workforce rather than simply fit into the current structure?

2. **Looking inward.** How hard are you looking? How do you feel about the process of evaluating your current search routines as well as your thoughts, feelings, and behaviors?

3. **What if?** What if external "others" perceive your company as looking only through door #1 and #2? What if those others you are hiring are cycling right back out? What would that say about your organization?

4. **Activity.** Examine your "doors" of hiring and promotion. Look past hiring trends to see what doors have historically been opened. Are they limited to just a few? Are there other doors that should be considered? What types of measures could be put in place to ensure a broader, more comprehensive search?

5. **This week's assignment.** Establish one new search routine. Search with sincerity and be persistent. As an example, identify and partner with a local organization that has developed inroads into the populations of people you would like to see at your organization. Begin creating relationships that can open doors for all involved.

| 32 |

A Late Start

After nearly 25 years of saying "I wish I could play the guitar," I actually am trying to learn how. It's part of my strategic life plan to inject inner turmoil every now and then via a new endeavor. Thanks to this particular endeavor, I find my plan is working out quite well: Inner turmoil and I are good friends at the moment.

Playing the guitar looks so easy—when someone else is doing it. My inaccurate perception of the skill it takes to play the guitar is a significant reason I put off learning for so long. I mistakenly believed that I could just pick it up at any time. "Guess again, buddy," say the guitar gods.

The guitar gods, overseers of guitars and guitar playing, make up the guitar rules. They are the ones who decided there would be six strings on a guitar (though they later passed an amendment allowing 12 strings). They also ordained that anyone who seeks guitar enlightenment will endure months of raw, painful fingertips followed by a loss of feeling in those same fingertips for the rest of one's life and maybe beyond.

To ensure that the guitar-playing world would be filled with people of utmost dedication, the guitar gods made the process of learning the art as painful as possible. Initially, to convert nonplayers, they made guitar playing fairly simple, though still painful. Any and all songs could be played with five chords: C, D, E, G, and A. With just a little practice, the finger placements required to play these chords are relatively easy to master. But then the gods created new, evil chords such as B and F-sharp, and the most evil chords of all, bar chords. The difficulty of playing these chords, which require a guitarist to be double-jointed and have the grip strength of an Austrian-born actor-turned-governor, stopped many folks in their tracks. The people could not understand why these new chords were necessary. But they endured the pain and discomfort.

Many hear the call to play the guitar, but only a few are chosen. Of course, I want to be among the chosen. I've wanted membership in this group for a long time and have actually pursued it several times, though halfheartedly. I never fully committed, and as a result I am currently trying to jump the B and F-sharp chord hurdles, with painfully slow progress. Even with this momentary stall, however, this time I will not stop. I will not fail. I will not take shortcuts.

I must admit it is tough to maneuver my fingers into the proper positioning for chords such as B. Now approaching 40, I find that my hands don't work with the exacting precision they once did. I'm not sure if the signals my brain sends are a bit corrupted or if my hands are getting back at me for years of blistering them up as a youngster playing tennis. Either way, it's taking me a long time to learn to play at even the simplest level, and the dexterity I had in younger days has locked itself in some safety box to which my brain has lost the key.

I knew from the beginning that buying a nice, expensive guitar would motivate me to endure the tough times. So I did, and it has helped. It's tougher to just give up when you've made a substantial investment. And, as it turns out, once you purchase a guitar, you need guitar-related paraphernalia. So, after the initial guitar purchase, I of course made frequent trips to the local guitar shop, always leaving with something in hand. Since my guitar was an "acoustic-electric" model, meaning it could be played with or without an amplifier, I was compelled to purchase an amplifier. Then I had to buy a cord. And because the amplifier has an additional input for a microphone, naturally I had to get a microphone and the necessary cord. Additional trips equipped me with an electronic tuner; assorted picks, guitar books, and learning DVDs; a music stand; a microphone stand; a stand for my guitar; a stand for my amplifier; a stand for my amplifier's stand...you get the picture. I rationalized all these purchases with a philosophy similar to that of Billy Crystal's character Fernando from *Saturday Night Live:* "It is better to look good than to play good." And look good I do. Is there anything sexier than a little Asian guy strapped to a guitar about half his size, surrounded by a mountain of stands? Didn't think so.

Okay, back to reality. I have often wondered how well I might be playing the guitar right now if I had started learning as a teenager. I'm sure I would have mastered it quickly. I had much more on my side then: more time, more nimble fingers, and more motivation. (I was under the impression that no matter how unsightly you might be, you could get girls if you played the guitar—kind of like Willie Nelson.) I would have saved a lot of money as well, primarily because at that time I didn't have much money to spend and because the guitar stuff that was available at the time is probably just a fraction of the equipment available today. But here I am, more than two decades later, struggling to scrunch my fingers into positions not meant for human hands. Nonetheless, I press on because if I don't start now, I'll be writing a similar story 10 years from now. Wouldn't that be a shame?

When Will You Start?

With my late start on the guitar in mind, I ask you how your inclusion and diversity initiatives are coming along, if at all. Have you and your organization made a full commitment to persevere even when tough hurdles arise? Do you have lots of things you have wanted to do but just haven't?

I recently participated in a community discussion that touched on the idea of "growing our own." Many commented that a lack of diversity made it difficult to attract and retain professionals of color. One person said her company had had the idea more than 10 years ago to engage children of color while they were still in junior high school, to introduce them to the business and teach them about a profession that continues to lack people of color and women. Others chimed in, saying that they had had similar ideas but had never truly pursued them. I asked what it might be like today if they had committed to a "grow our own" initiative. All were silent for a moment, but you could tell they were thinking.

Okay, so you have some good ideas but haven't started to act on them. What are you going to do about that now, with the unstoppable thrust of an increasingly diverse world in your face? What if you were to start now? Could you be reaping the rewards in a few years? It might take longer than that, but you'll never know if you don't start—with full commitment.

"I coulda been a contenda" if only I had started playing the guitar years ago. How will your organization contend in the future if you don't take a serious look at inclusion and diversity issues now? If yours is one of those organizations that fully committed years ago, congratulations. You have a big head start on many. If you are still spinning your wheels, I suggest you start putting your ideas into action. Playing the guitar is still a matter of choice for me. Being a diverse, inclusive, and culturally competent organization is no longer a choice for organizations. It is an imperative.

How good at inclusion and diversity could you be in five years if you started in earnest today? With continued blessings from the guitar gods, I plan to play the guitar well in five years. I'm passionate about the guitar. I have an unwavering commitment to play well. And I have made a substantial financial investment. Can you and your organization say similar things when it comes to inclusion and diversity?

Beginning Now

Whether you're just starting or continuing the journey, your efforts can always be amplified. To help you think about how your organization might ramp up its efforts, here are some questions to ask, an activity, and an assignment for this week.

1. **First glance.** What efforts has your organization made around inclusion and diversity? When did you start? What have the results been?

2. **Looking inward.** Are you fully committed to change? Do you like the idea of a diverse workforce and have a heartfelt commitment to inclusion? How are you demonstrating your commitment?

3. **What if?** What if your organization had started its efforts five years sooner than it did? What would the results have been compared to what they are? What if you started practicing inclusion right now? What would the results be five years from now?

4. **Activity.** List your organization's past and present diversity efforts both in hiring and in changing corporate culture, along with when they began. Has participation in training been primarily optional? What should your leaders do to demonstrate that they value diverse backgrounds and perspectives? List some additional ways your company could start requiring participation and accountability. Take some cues from other "players" that are further along in their implementation.

5. **This week's assignment.** Commit! Practice! Begin mastering a new chord today by playing notes on the individual strings of your organizational guitar to produce a sweet-sounding chord. As an idea, practice acknowledging everyone you come in contact with in your workplace by using his or her first name. If you don't know someone's name, learn it!

33

I Hate Board Games

There I was, minding my own business at another family get-together. Dinner was settling nicely in my tummy, giving me that glazed-over, sleepy feeling, and I was just this side of blissful rapid eye movement when I heard the dreaded words: "Let's play board games!"

To me, these are not normal, everyday words. They form a sentence that elicits a visceral response. I can't bear to hear them. I fear my "Mr. Hyde" will show himself.

"Stop!" I screamed within the confines of my mind. But again the words attacked: "Anyone wanna play board games?"

I feigned sleep, hoping that enough players would be found without requiring my participation. On this occasion, I wanted to be the kid who gets picked last (or, better yet, not at all). I heard people stirring around me as they made their way to another room. Yes! I dared not peek at what was going on, but after a while it sounded like the coast was clear. The old spiritual reverberated in my head: "Free at last, free at last, thank God Almighty, I'm free at last!"

Then, out of nowhere, I felt a tap on my arm. I didn't react. That resulted in another tap. "Leave me alone," I wanted to say. But then I heard, "Wake up, Uncle Steve. We're going to play Monopoly!" The jig was up. Surrendering, I opened my eyes and saw my little nephew smiling at me: "Let's go, Uncle Steve!" Whose kid was this, anyway? "C'mon, they're starting, Uncle Steve." He was relentless. All I could think of was the Borg species from the *Star Trek: The Next Generation* series, aliens that assimilate all living beings into their "hivemind." Resistance was futile, so I got out of the La-Z-Boy and slunk off to prison, er, the game table. The Monopoly board was prepared.

To make matters worse, I was stuck with the thimble as my game piece. I couldn't be the race car or the shoe; I had to be the thimble. I had a bad attitude before the game even began, and I could see no way for the situation to improve. But something strange happened along the way. People started talking and laughing. My nephew told a joke, a bad one, but people laughed. I found myself laughing, too.

"Okay, this is not so bad," I thought. I was enjoying the game. Heck, I was even taking people's money! By the end of the game, my attitude about board games had changed completely. Well, maybe not completely, but I was on my way to becoming a board game advocate—so long as I didn't have to be the thimble.

How Are You Enlisting Players?

Many times we start out with a bad attitude about things we are asked to do. We don't want to do them, but somewhere along the way we discover that it's not that bad. Sometimes we even find ourselves enjoying the task or process, and in the end we walk away with a new and improved attitude.

I am often asked if I think diversity training should be required or voluntary. My typical response is, How important is inclusion to your organization? Does it make sense to value all of your human resources? Does it make your organization better and more competitive when your workforce embraces and values inclusion and diversity in an increasingly global society?

Think for a minute about why training is required in various areas of your organization. Likely it's because the skills people acquire through the training benefit your organization. Why should it be any different with respect to training and education around inclusion and diversity? If inclusion and diversity are core values for your organization, if you believe that it's a good thing to have all employees feel valued and included (i.e., engaged), the answer to questions about diversity training is pretty clear.

Many organizations don't want to mandate diversity training because they believe that people have a bad attitude about it—that it will just make things worse. So diversity training becomes voluntary and the "choir" hears more preaching. Many people do have a negative mind-set about diversity training. However, the problem is not with the concept but with the way the training is presented—that is, with the way the leadership prepares the organization for that type of training. Diversity training must be framed within the context of continuous organization improvement. It must be sold as a benefit to everyone. This starts with leadership and flows to every part of the organization.

People's bad attitudes toward diversity training likely will change when they see how the training can benefit both them and the organization. Contrary to conventional wisdom, behavior does not always stem from attitude. Sometimes, behavior can have a powerful impact on changing someone's attitude. Negative attitudes about diversity training can be changed through training if the training is done well. Who knows? Maybe those who once viewed diversity as I viewed board games will find themselves enjoying the process—and gaining a strategic advantage, too!

Ideally, your organization is providing inclusion and diversity training and education, and framing it in such a way that your people see it as vital to the organization. If the leaders of your organization are not communicating to the employees that such training is about organization development, about total employee engagement, about creativity and innovation, about continuous improvement, then don't be surprised if you hear lots of negative rumblings about diversity training.

Teaching People How to Play

Properly framing training is key in getting people to engage in something they may perceive as negative. To help you discover how you might frame inclusion and diversity training better, here are some questions to ask, an activity, and an assignment for this week.

1. **First glance.** How does your organization prepare people for inclusion and diversity training? Can it be framed differently in order to change people's perceptions and expectations? Is it presented as an opportunity or a chore? Is it required or optional?

2. **Looking inward.** Do you personally approach inclusion and diversity training with resistance or as an opportunity to stretch your learning? If it's the latter, why? If it's the former, why?

3. **What if?** What if your organization reframed inclusion and diversity training? What if such training could be fun, challenging, and insightful all at the same time? What if you really did include creative, enjoyable games as part of the training?

4. **Activity.** Identify three or four enjoyable activities for the workplace that could expand your group's knowledge about other cultures—for example, book clubs, movies, festivals, or discussion groups. Creatively explore how these opportunities might be communicated and supported throughout the organization.

Teaching People How to Play (cont'd)

5. **This week's assignment.** Engage in a fun and enjoyable activity that could teach participants about inclusion- and diversity-related issues. For example, you might play a *Jeopardy*-type game that gets at demographic shifts currently underway.

| 34 |

The Power of Magnification

When I was a youngster growing up in California, I spent much of my summer vacation playing outside. For some reason, I had a lot of interest in nature and science, so I caught a lot of insects. Up until my seventh birthday I was relatively nice to the bugs I captured. Yes, occasionally I would "mishandle" a bug to the point that it would die, or I would turn an eight-legged creature into a six-legged one. But heck, why be a little kid if you can't experiment with bugs? Though I held a number of funerals for the little creatures that didn't survive my operating table, for the most part I took the Hippocratic oath rather seriously. That is, until I turned seven.

On my seventh birthday I received something I vaguely recall as a "science kit." This thing was cool to a 7-year-old. Heck, it would be cool to a 37-year-old. It had a microscope, tweezers, plastic test tubes, and a bunch of other stuff. But what I really liked was the magnifying glass. I remember thinking that whoever had invented this thing must have been a genius. With a magnifying glass I could make a little Oreo cookie

217

look huge. The cookie didn't fill up my tummy any better, but it looked like it would. I could see the tiniest details on my dog's face. Hair follicles sure look funny up close. But the best thing was examining the bugs I caught. If you've ever seen a grasshopper's head up close, you can understand the pure joy such a sight can give a 7-year-old.

My wrong turn down the road of bug cruelty began several days after my birthday. It was, as usual, a hot and sunny day in Southern California. I thought, "What a great day to go outside with my new magnifying glass to look for bugs." Little did I know my fall from grace was close at hand—that I would soon morph into the Hannibal Lecter of the bug kingdom. Unfortunately for the potato bugs that lived under a board near our apartment, I began with them. I wanted to look at them up close. If you think potato bugs are ugly to the naked eye, wait until you get them under a magnifying glass. It's a good ugly, though.

A curious thing happened as I examined the potato bugs. With one big one under scrutiny, I pulled my head away to peer at another creature and, in doing so, let the sun shine into the magnifying glass. It put a nice little spotlight on the bug, and, as I tried to focus once again on the bug, I saw that the spotlight got bigger or smaller depending on the distance between the magnifying glass and the bug. I also noticed that as the spotlight got smaller, there was much more movement by the bug. I pursued this newfound correlation with great interest.

Eventually, after a series of adjustments, I had a highly concentrated, bright dot on the bug. Soon after, smoke began to rise from the creature, accompanied by a slight sizzling sound. The bug's hurried movements to get away told me that this was not an enjoyable experience for him, but I followed with my magnifying glass anyway, and it did not take long for the bug to stop moving. With the light still concentrated on the back of the bug, it caught fire. Way cool!

I spent what seemed like hours finding and roasting bugs. Then my mom found me. Suffice it to say, that was the end of my bug-burning days. How can life be fair when a 7-year-old can't enjoy a day in the sun with bugs and a magnifying glass? Melting plastic army men would have to do.

How Are You Focusing Your Energies?

The lesson here comes from the power of a magnifying glass to focus light onto an object. The magnifying glass takes incoherent, or unorganized, light particles and directs them in such a way that a very tight, concentrated, and powerful beam is produced. Without a magnifying glass or other similar tool, light particles remain unorganized, diffused, and weak.

Do the last three adjectives describe your organization's diversity initiatives? I often have observed that when organizations try to address every possible dimension of diversity (because they don't want to leave anyone out), they dilute the entire process. Sometimes they do so much that they become satisfied in the doing and put little emphasis on the outcome. Or employees may latch on to a particular dimension of diversity with which they are most comfortable and use it as a proxy for being comfortable with all dimensions.

Emphasizing one or two dimensions of diversity can enable an organization to focus its resources and accomplish more than it could with a diffused approach. Does this mean that the organization can forget about other dimensions of diversity? Absolutely not! It means that the organization has a primary focus on one or two dimensions it has deemed vitally important while still addressing other diversity issues. (It's important not to forget those other issues, because people who fully embrace one type of diversity—for example, gender diversity—may think they are okay with all dimensions, when in fact they have not come to grips with racial or ethnic diversity, sexual orientation, or religion. If they think this way, they rarely see the value of committing to diversity efforts.)

Different organizations may have different areas of focus. Some, on the basis of research results and changing demographics, may feel that gender diversity is most important. Others, on the basis of their location, may choose racial or ethnic diversity. Still others may choose generational diversity because of the makeup of their workforce. Just as an organization must be careful to communicate why it plans to focus on one aspect of its business more than another—for example, customer service versus marketing—it must communicate the rationale behind emphasizing certain dimensions of diversity. This difference in emphasis does not mean that marketing will be forgotten. Rather, it says that at this particular time the data suggest that customer satisfaction requires greater attention if the organization expects to be successful in the future.

If your organization is committed to inclusion and diversity, it may help to think of exclusion and discrimination as big, ugly bugs. In doing so, you can think of your strategic diversity plan as a giant magnifying glass that can either shine a diffused beam on all of the bugs or focus resources to obliterate them one by one. Why have a weak, diffused approach to inclusion and diversity when you can leverage the power of focus and magnification?

Magnifying Your Efforts

Could your energy and resources be better focused on issues of inclusion and diversity? To help you focus a powerful beam on the ugly bugs of exclusion and narrow-mindedness, here are some questions to ask, an activity, and an assignment for this week.

1. **First glance.** What are your organization's big, ugly bugs? What kinds of impacts (financial, social, cultural, and so on) have they had?

2. **Looking inward.** Turn your magnification inward. Identify your own big, ugly bugs.

3. **What if?** What if you don't have the proper magnification to see the bugs? How can you see them more clearly or get help in doing so? What if you see pretty bugs when others see ugly ones?

4. **Activity.** Work together (in a diverse group representing many perspectives!) to identify the top 10 big, ugly bugs in your organization. Prioritize these bugs, listing the potential results if they were eliminated. Develop a strategic plan to tackle the top three. Include a time line, steps necessary to achieve these goals, and indicators that will demonstrate (to you and others) that you are on the right path. Hold one another accountable with regular check-in points and updates. *Note:* You may discover that your ugliest bugs have little to do with traditional dimensions of diversity. For example, poor communication is not often seen as a diversity issue, but it can have a powerful impact on inclusion and diversity.

Magnifying Your Efforts (cont'd)

5. **This week's assignment.** Focus your magnifying glass on one of your big, ugly bugs and start to get rid of it. For example, critically examine the way you and others may subtly devalue people through common communication behaviors.

| 35 |

More Cookies

My eldest son, Nicholas, loves Oreo cookies. Let me qualify that. If there is an Oreo anywhere near, Nicholas no doubt will be among the first to make claim. Such was the case during a recent family dinner.

Like many concerned about the decline of the family, we make it a point to sit down together for dinner. It gives us time to talk about our day and build family unity without distractions. When we ate out recently, fortunately for us, the restaurant's kitchen staff was a little slow, giving us even more time around the dinner table. And that brings us back to the Oreos.

Nicholas had just finished a very healthy dinner of a hot dog and french fries when something on the dessert menu caught his eye: the 7-year-old's Holy Grail, a vanilla sundae topped with two Oreos. There was no need to look at the rest of the menu—Nicholas knew what he wanted. The waitress, obviously an Oreo lover herself, seemed to know, too. The order was placed without words.

Nicholas' eyes lit up like fireflies on a warm summer night when the waitress brought out his sundae, and he was ready to launch an all-out assault on the cookies that lay on top. But just as he reached for the first Oreo, a voice from across the table interrupted: "Can I have an Oreo, Nicholas?" Younger brother Jacob had fired a verbal challenge at Nicholas' sense of brotherly love. Silence blanketed the table as Nicholas paused to consider Jacob's request. I waited anxiously to see if my wife and I had raised a son who would put others ahead of himself.

Like many other Oreo lovers, Nicholas is most passionate not about the entire cookie, but about the creamy middle. After what seemed like minutes, he tried some creative negotiation: "Jacob, how 'bout you have the outside after I eat the white stuff inside?" I'm sure his politeness masked a wish that his parents had taken birth control more seriously following his arrival in the world.

But Jacob would not settle for just part of an Oreo. He restated his plea with a pathetic cry. Nicholas looked to me, hoping I would intervene. But as a *Star Trek* fan, I stayed true to the Prime Directive: I would not interfere in the lives of these lower life forms we call children. Besides, watching Nicholas struggle with an obvious moral dilemma was getting to be fun.

"But, Jacob, if I give you the whole cookie, I'll only have one left," Nicholas reasoned. He had not realized that younger brothers are not rational beings. A higher life form might actually care about how another feels, but clearly this young one was not so evolved. After minutes of pleading, the good in Nicholas broke through—kind of. "Okay, you can have the cookie. But I get one of yours next time." Nicholas handed over the Oreo and somberly began eating his remaining cookie.

The waitress had been watching from afar, and as Nicholas finished she came by and asked him what was wrong. Nicholas was in no mood to talk, but he responded anyway. "I only got one Oreo." She stepped closer to Nicholas and told him she had seen how nice he had been to his brother. And as she commended him for sharing with a pat on the head, she put a dish with two more Oreos on the table in front of him. The light returned to his eyes. He softly thanked his newfound Oreo angel and turned to me. "Look, Dad, she gave me two more Oreos. I gave my brother a cookie and I got two back."

"That's cool!" I said, putting out my hand to receive a high five.

Nicholas smacked my hand. "Yep, real cool," he replied. "You're right, Dad, sharing is a good thing."

Are You Sharing Your Oreos?

Sharing is a good thing. What a wonderful lesson for a child to learn. It's also a great lesson for adults to learn and put into practice.

Often, people view inclusion and diversity as a zero-sum endeavor. That is, there are finite "goodies" out there, and giving up some of them means having fewer to enjoy. For some, sharing power and control and allowing others in on the decision-making process only means "I will have less." In other words, if I give up one of my cookies, it means I have less dessert. What these same people don't understand is that giving up 10 percent of their Oreos might help create even more rewards. While they might own a smaller percentage of the dessert, the new amount will be greater in size than the original one or two cookies. Indeed, what if it's not a zero-sum game? What if everybody gains when we put others before ourselves?

Allowing more—and more diverse—people to contribute where

they previously were not included will bring advantages to organizations in an increasingly diverse future. Organizations that handle diversity strategically (read: share dessert for all to benefit) will have a great advantage over those that do not. Likely they will grow, while others will stagnate.

Putting too much energy into preserving one's personal goodies often has the ironic effect of endangering the enterprise that provided the goodies in the first place. Put that enterprise in enough danger because its leadership is not willing to share and include, and it ultimately will decline, if not disintegrate. I would argue that sharing control of a structurally sound, dynamic ship is much better than having total control of a dilapidated, sinking one. As Nicholas would surely attest, 75 percent of four Oreos is immensely better than having 100 percent of two Oreos. Truly, sharing is a good thing.

How to Increase Your Organization's Oreos

To help you put into practice the notion of sharing, here are some questions to ask, an activity, and an assignment for this week.

1. **First glance.** Who has the Oreos in your organization? What measures have you seen your leaders take to keep their cookies? To share them?

2. **Looking inward.** What Oreos do you have, and where did you get them? What could you gain by sharing your Oreos? What cookies do you have that you fear losing?

3. **What if?** What if more people in your organization shared their Oreos? What if, because of the sharing, the number of cookies doubled? What might cookie sharing look like in terms of hiring, development, retention, and work culture?

4. **Activity.** Form a group of five or six people. Go around the group and inventory each person's personal Oreos, including skills, knowledge, experiences, access, mentors, opportunities, and so on. Which of those cookies do you wish you had? Who has them? Discuss ways in which the group's participants could partner with one another to share cookies. Are there mentoring partnerships that could be formed? Invitations to special meetings that could be extended? Introductions to higher-level executives? Sharing of experiences and lessons learned? Identify steps you can take to share your resources, knowledge, or leadership access with others in your organization. What might be some tangible benefits for them? For you?

How to Increase Your Organization's Oreos (cont'd)

5. **This week's assignment.** Share one or more of your Oreos with others. Try inviting people who rarely get included to meetings, activities, events, and so on.

36

Lion Chase

"Let's play lion chase." That's the greeting my three sons gave me the other night as I entered our house after a long day of work. It wasn't, "Hi, Dad, we love you, glad you're home," or, "Hi, Dad, you're the greatest, how was your day?" It wasn't even a simple "Hi, Dad." It was perfectly clear that at this particular moment they were missing a piece from their play puzzle, and that piece had just walked through the door.

But I didn't want to play lion chase, which is a tiring game. The game had begun with our first son, Nicholas, as soon as he started gaining some upright mobility. I would chase him around the house on my hands and knees, doing my best imitation of a lion. It wasn't a very good imitation, but it didn't have to be because it's really not that difficult to delight a 1-year-old. When the game started, I was a bit younger with a little more energy, a little more time, and better knees. Now, well, let's just say I'm a little more "mature."

I tried to get out of playing lion chase, reeling off a number of rational excuses for why I couldn't play and hoping they would understand.

They didn't. "I'm tired, guys. Maybe later," was my first feeble attempt to resist. This never works. I don't even know why I bother. Nicholas, my 7-year-old, looked at me, smiled, and fired back, "Yeah, right, Dad." Where is the respect for elders Vietnamese kids are supposed to have? Who's teaching this kid, anyway?

Then 5-year-old Zachary chimed in: "C'mon Dad, we want to play lion chase." Accompanying his words were a leg hug and fake smile that broke down my defenses. Zachary is a smart little bugger with the emotional intelligence of someone greater in years—and he knows how to use it.

Jacob, the youngest son, waited patiently on the left flank, behind a door, looking for an opening to join the first wave of attack. Zachary looked back at Jacob and seamlessly moved his hug from my left leg to my right. That was Jacob's signal to move forward. With reckless abandon he surged ahead, his radar locked in on my left leg. He sounded the battle cry, "D-A-D-D-Y." The impact of the hit rocked me back on my heels.

Sensing that the objective was within reach, Nicholas said, "If you play lion chase, we'll clean our rooms." Then, just as I was about to surrender, Mom arrived.

My wife gave both warring parties an unconditional directive. "Shh, you're too loud, Natalie is sleeping." My sons quickly quieted down. "Stop arguing, go outside, and play lion chase there. Steve, go ahead—you know you're going to do it anyway." Mom added by way of incentive, "Natalie hasn't had a nap all day. If you wake her up, boys, you'll have to go to your rooms for some quiet time." A tense stillness came over the room.

Satisfied that her message had been received, Mom left the room. But knowing her sons well, she quickly returned with three simple but forceful words: "I mean it." She reinforced the words with a stare and a nod of her head.

Nicholas, Zachary, and I recognized that Mom was not in the best of moods. History had taught the older males in the family that it's best not to mess with Mom during these times. But in Jacob's still-developing 3-year-old brain, the connection between actions and consequences had not yet fused. As Nicholas, Zachary, and I began to leave the room, Jacob again locked onto my left leg while pleading, "LET'S PLAY LION CHASE."

"This is not good, not good at all," I thought. You see, being the third son, Jacob had to find ways to attract attention. So over the course of time he had learned to be loud. In fact, he had developed two settings for oral communication—loud and LOUDER. And he had no mute button. On this occasion, his outburst spelled doom. Theoretically, there is nothing faster than the speed of light, but Mom's return to the room challenged that notion. "I told you what would happen. Down to your rooms, boys."

Nicholas and Zachary protested, "We didn't do anything. It was Jacob. He's the one being loud. It's not fair, we didn't..." Recognizing the futility of their attempts to influence Mom, I interrupted midsentence. "Go to your rooms, guys. Now's not the time." If you think I intervened to shield my sons from further consequences, you have it all wrong. I did it purely for self-preservation. I suffer when my wife is not in a good mood, no matter who is the cause. When Mom is not at her best, we are in a "No" environment: no joy, no fun, no communication, and no you-know-what.

As I walked my sons down to their rooms, I felt a little bad that I hadn't just played lion chase with them when they first asked. To ease my guilt, I told them I would play lion chase with them after Natalie woke up from her nap...and after they cleaned their rooms. With that offer, smiles reappeared on their faces and they raced to their rooms to begin cleaning.

Do You Need a Diversity Mom?

If you are a part of inclusion and diversity initiatives in your organization, you know that resistance to those programs is inevitable. You and others are like my sons trying to make me play lion chase—pushing and pulling others to join the organization's inclusion efforts. And there are always people who resist. You try to get their buy-in and commitment, but they refuse to listen. Or, if they do listen, they don't hear. They have feeble excuses based on poor, outdated information. They often aren't willing even to open their minds to the possibility that a more inclusive organization benefits everyone—for example, through increased employee engagement and enthusiasm and enhanced creativity and innovation.

This battle, which often takes place at middle and lower levels, makes the organization vulnerable in many areas. It is at this time that the leadership of the organization needs to communicate clearly the benefits of action and the consequences of inaction, just as my wife made clear to us the consequences of not complying with her directive. All parties involved suffer. Maybe it's just some people who suffer in the short term, but it's all of us in the long term.

Organizations that aren't making progress with their inclusion and diversity initiatives will, in a more diverse future, find themselves losing momentum. Competitors who have embraced inclusion and diversity will be better able to attract and retain the best and brightest. They'll be in a better position to resolve vexing problems because of the diversity of perspectives and cumulative cognitive powers they possess. And they'll also be in a better position to defend themselves when the outside environment turns hostile. These organizations are more likely to hold their position when the economy sours. When other organizations are losing market share because they don't take seriously the bottom-line impact of changing demographics, these organizations will find creative ways to take advantage of the changes. For example, they will be better able to capitalize on a people-of-color market that represents nearly two trillion dollars' worth of collective buying power; and on a gay and lesbian population that represents an increasingly affluent, better educated, and more powerful consumer force; and on an aging population that is a gold mine of wisdom, stability, and buying power.

Better-prepared organizations are less likely to find themselves fending off discrimination lawsuits and dealing with high employee turnover rates, both of which negatively and significantly affect an organization's efficiency and bottom line. When others are laying off, these organizations are retaining, even hiring.

So the message is clear. Everyone—the entire organization—benefits when the organization is inclusive and open to diverse perspectives. Alternatively, everyone suffers when the organization is relatively homogeneous and exclusive. While the message is clear, sometimes it requires the intervention of a powerful leadership to get it through the thick skulls of those who don't want to "play lion chase." Sometimes your organization needs an Inclusion and Diversity Mom to get the message through. Does your organization have an Inclusion and Diversity Mom who can effectively communicate the consequences of inaction with respect to inclusion and diversity? If it doesn't, it had better get one.

Every organization needs an Inclusion and Diversity Mom.

Getting Mom Involved

To help you identify and make the best use of your organization's Diversity Mom, here are some questions to ask, an activity, and an assignment for this week.

1. **First glance.** Who is the Inclusion and Diversity Mom in your organization? What did that person do when there was resistance to your diversity initiatives?

2. **Looking inward.** Can you remember a time when you reacted badly to a message from your organization's Inclusion and Diversity Mom? Why did you react as you did? What happened?

3. **What if?** What if you were the Inclusion and Diversity Mom and you saw a world around you with changing demographics, a global marketplace, and an increasingly diverse workforce? What would you say to your "kids" to let them know that embracing difference and inclusion is a serious imperative?

4. **Activity.** On a flip chart, mark two columns labeled "Impact A" and "Impact B." Use column A to outline the benefits your company will reap as a result of engaging its increasingly diverse demographics. In column B, outline the impact of staying homogeneous. Think beyond just the first couple of years to the long-term cause and effect. How might your Inclusion and Diversity Mom clearly communicate the tangible benefits of action and the unavoidable consequences of inaction? How would she get her message through the thick skulls of the organization?

5. **This week's assignment.** Listen to your Inclusion and Diversity Mom and step outside your comfort zone. As an example, why not volunteer to participate in an upcoming diversity- and inclusion-related event sponsored by the organization?

"Life is a journey of error correction. Are you humble enough to admit your mistakes and courageous enough to correct them?"
—**Steve L. Robbins**

About the Author

Born in Vietnam, Steve L. Robbins immigrated to the United States with his mother in 1970, when he was 5 years old. He and his mother faced and overcame many obstacles as immigrants in their new land during a time when there was much anti-Vietnamese sentiment. Working through and rising out of the challenges of poverty, discrimination, and the tough streets of Los Angeles, Robbins received his BA degree in communication with honors from Calvin College and his MA and PhD degrees in communication science from Michigan State University.

After working stints at ABC Sports in Chicago; as a news producer at the NBC affiliate in Grand Rapids, Michigan; and director of the Woodrick Institute for the Study of Diversity and Racism at Aquinas College, Robbins founded S. L. Robbins & Associates, a consultancy specializing in the areas of inclusion, leadership, and the power of caring. Working with for-profit and not-for-profit organizations of all sizes, the company offers guidance on these and myriad other issues that are increasingly affecting organizations in a global world and marketplace.

In his speaking and consulting work, Robbins brings his insightful perspectives on human behavior in general, and inclusion and diversity specifically, to myriad companies and audiences. His research-based approach uses the science of human behavior and cognitive neuroscience to invite individuals and organizations into curious and crucial conversations on the power of belonging. Drawing on his compelling life journey, his talks and workshops are filled with intriguing stories, laugh-out-loud humor, and a keen understanding of the human condition. A highly sought-after keynote speaker, Robbins has worked with numerous organizations, including Disney, Pixar, Walmart, Toyota, Hulu, Boeing, Microsoft, Coca-Cola, Lululemon, NASA, the US Navy, US Treasury Department, Michelin, Paypal, and numerous other for-profit and not-for-profit entities.

Recently, Robbins launched S2S Studios, a visual storytelling studio to provide video-based training resources to organizations. S2S (Something2Say) Studios is an all-women-run studio with the mission of providing high-quality narrative storytelling to positively impact the world. S2S Studios welcomes you to join in our mission of using visual stories to move hearts and minds to move people and the world in a more positive direction.

To learn more about Robbins and S. L. Robbins & Associates (www.SLRobbins.com) and S2S Studios(www.s2s-studios.com), please visit their respective websites.